NFT GUIDE

How to Create and Sell Non Fungible Tokens, discover Crypto Art and Collectibles as Crypto Assets

Table of Contents

INTRODUCTION..04

CHAPTER ONE...05

   What is a non-financial token (NFT)?....................05
   Working of NFTs?..06
   How worthy NFTs Is?..08
   The Opportunities with NFTs...............................13
   Are NFT Stocks The Right Investment For You?..........13

CHAPTER TWO...14

   Will NFTs Be the Future of Modern Art?..................14
   How NFTs Are Shaking Up the Art World?.................15
   Defining the Crypto Art Movement.........................22

CHAPTER THREE..25

   How to Buy NFTs..25

CHAPTER FOUR..30

   Block chain - For Normal People............................30
   Steganography in Principle...................................33
   Reasons Why You Should Buy Paintings 35
   Seven Easy Tips for Selling Your Art......................38
   How to Start Selling Art.......................................40

CHAPTER FIVE..42
  What Are Crypto Assets?...42
  What Are Assets in Accounting?..................................44
  Characteristics of Crypto Assets..................................48
  The Key Is to Get in Early..50
  Secrets on Security: A Gentle overview 53

CHAPTER SIX..57
  Crypto currency: The Fintech Disruptor.....................67
  Crypto TREND...69

CHAPTER SEVEN...72
  Digital Assets and Crypto Assets.................................75
  Top Indications You Need a Digital Asset....................80

CONCLUSION...83

INTRODUCTION

Investing directly in Crypto Currency (CC) requires the use of new tools and the adoption of some new concepts, which can be intimidating for the traditional investor. So, if you do decide to dip your toes into this market, make sure you know exactly what you're doing and what to expect.

To buy and sell CCs, you must first find an exchange that deals in the products you want to buy and sell, whether it's Bit coin, Lite coin, or any of the other over 1300 tokens available. We've briefly described the products and services available at a few exchanges in previous editions to give you an idea of what's available.

Crypto trading can be profitable if you keep an eye on the market. You may, however, find it difficult at times. Fortunately, if you require assistance, crypto signal services are available. They can be used to make the right decision at the right time using the signals they provide. There are numerous service providers from which to choose. A few pointers to help you choose the best one are provided below.

NFTs (non-fungible tokens) are a type of crypto currency asset where each item, or token, is unique. As a result, they are useless as a currency but extremely useful for other purposes, such as crypto art. Continue reading to learn more.

CHAPTER ONE

What is a non-financial token (NFT)?

When we say something is fungible, we're referring to the fact that each unit can be swapped out. A unit of currency, for example, is fungible. When you exchange one dollar for another, you essentially have the same thing. A one-of-a-kind work of art, other affect is, they can't be replicate. A digital artwork, a video clip, a gif, a tweet, or even a digital trading card can all be considered NFTs. Anything digital, really, but, there is a huge current/energy to buzz is about using the technology require to selling the art containing digitally.
Why is it so hot at the moment? We saw digital artist Beeple sell a piece of artwork for $69 million and Twitter founder Jack Dorsey's tweet for $2.9 million. These are a few of the reasons why NFTs are so popular at the moment.

What exactly is an NFT?

Non-fungible token
That doesn't help things any.
Sorry for the inconvenience. Non-fungible it actually means it is special and cannot be replaced by anything else. Bitcoin, for example, can be considered, which means you can exchange and get the same thing. A unique trading card, too, cannot be duplicated. You can find something completely interesting if you can switch to another card.

The term "non-fungible token" refers to a token that is not fungible. In financial matters, a visual aid is a component of units, such as money.

For cash, you can sell a £ 10 note for two £ 5 notes and have the same amount.

This is unthinkable if something does not work, which means that there are some kinds of things that end up being exchanged separately.

It could be a home or a unique art creation, for example, the Mona Lisa. You can take a picture of an art creation or buy a print, but there will always be one different drawing.

In the developed world, NFTs are "different" resources that can be bought and sold as some other asset; however, they have no real structure.

Advanced tokens can measure access to testaments for real or virtual resources.

Working of NFTs?

The types of art that can be purchased as NFTs are virtually endless. It doesn't end there after Dorsey's tweet. Sophia the Robot's NFT Artwork sold for nearly $700,000. The New York Times column's crypto tokens sold for $560,000. The beauty of NFTs is that they can be uploaded to an NFT marketplace once they've been created. Panting and other common objects to set up the show is important in terms of the fact that they are the same type.

Computer records, too, can be copied effectively and efficiently.

The technology can be "softened" by the NFTs to create a patent that can be purchased and sold carefully.

Will just advanced exchange cards eventually produce a variety of cards?

A record of who owns it, such as a cryptographic currency, is placed on a standard record known as a blockchain.
On a proof-of-work blockchain, its unique identity and ownership are then verified. This is the same technology that underpins most currencies that are know and popular are BTC & Ethereal, and other well-known coins. The Ethereum platform is used by the majority of NFTs, but there is growing interest in using Cardano and Polkadot's platforms instead. This explains why Cardano and Polkadot have recently made significant gains in the crypto space.

Since the lumberjack is kept up by a great many PCs around the world, records can't be made.

NFTs can likewise go into keen agreements, for instance, that give the craftsman a rebate on any future symbolic deals.

What keeps individuals from emulating computerized craftsmanship?

Nothing. Human workmanship, sold at the rate of $ 69 million, has been seen by a large number of individuals, and the picture has been replicated and dispersed many occasions over.

Much of the time, the craftsman holds the copyright of their work, permitting them to keep creating and selling duplicates.
However, the purchaser of the NFT receives a "token" proving ownership of the "original" work.

It's been compared to purchasing an autographed print by some.

Millions of dollars are being paid for tokens?
Yes, indeed. It's just as crazy as it sounds.

How do NFTs work?
Many NFTs, at an important level, are part of the Ethereum blockchain. Ethereum, like bitcoin and dogecoin, is a digital currency; however, its blockchain similarly supports these NFTs, which store additional data that allows them to operate differently from the ETH currency. It is important that some blockchains can use NFTs in their specific ways.

What should you buy at the NFT supermarket?
NFTs can areas, that can be possibility of anything can be digital (drawings, music, even your brain being download at maximum rates , which after that turned into Artificially, but these are the current buzz is focused on using the technology selling all related having digital arts.

Do you mean people paying for my good tweets?
My believe is not of anyone will be able to stop so that you can't proceed more, but that the thing, which I mean's. A lot of the discussion revolves around NFTs, but only in the context of digital art.

How worthy NFTs Is?

Hypothetically, anybody can make a sign of their work and sell it as an NFT, yet late articles on the offer of millions have made a benefit.

The energized Gif of Nyan Cat, the image of the 2011 flying feline image, sold more than $ 500,000 on February nineteenth.

Grimes sold a portion of his advanced workmanship for more than $ 6 million half a month later.

The workmanship isn't the solitary thing that is given a token and sold. With offers coming to up to $ 2.5 million, Twitter originator Jack Dorsey has advanced NFT's first tweet.

Christie's offer of NFT computerized craftsman for Beeple NFT for $ 69 million (£ 50 million) has set an elevated expectation for advanced workmanship.

Nonetheless, as digital currencies, there are worries about the effect of the blockchain on the environment.

Many people are even more pessimistic.
NFTs, according to David Gerard, is the writer of the Attack of the 50-foot containing Blockchain, is similar to buying "official collectibles" like trading cards.

"Some artists are absolutely making money on this stuff... but you probably won't," he cautioned.
He described the people selling the NFTs as "crypto-grifters."
"The same guys who've always been at it, trying to come up with a new type of worthless magic bean that they can sell for money," says the narrator.
The idea of holding and purchasing NFTs, "makes no sense."
"The idea of buying something that isn't there is just strange."
"I believe the investors are a bunch of jerks, but I hope they don't lose their money."

Do people really believe this will turn into a form of art collecting?
I'm certain a few groups earnestly trust in this way, similar to somebody who paid about $ 390,000 briefly Grimes video or

somebody who paid $ 6.6 million for a Beeple video. Truth be told, one of Beeple's works was sold at sell-off in Christie's, a world-renowned sales management firm.

Apologies, you were too bustling right-tapping on that Beeple video and downloading that record for which one paid a huge number of dollars.

Quit ridiculing. However, indeed, that is the place where circumstances become difficult. You can make however many duplicates of the computerized document as you need, including the craftsmanship that accompanies NFT.
NFTs, then again, they are intended to give you something that you won't go anyplace else: work proprietorship (albeit the craftsman can, in any case, hold copyright and propagation, for example, body workmanship). To put it another way, anybody can purchase a Monet print by gathering body workmanship. However, the original can only be owned by one person.

Without wishing to disparage Beeple, the video isn't quite a Monet.
What are your thoughts on the Gucci Ghost, which retails for $3,600? You also didn't allow me to finish earlier. Beeple's image was auctioned.
 Any individual who has gotten that Monet will actually want to see the value in it as an unmistakable article. A duplicate of computerized craftsmanship is what might be compared to the first. However, the freedom that comes with owning an original Beeple...

What is the point of this?
Whether, it upon you, you are writer or as buyer, it all depends.

I can say, I'm the best Artist!
First and foremost, I congratulate you. Congratulations on your accomplishment. You might be you are keen on NFTs in light of the fact that they permit you to sell a task that would be hard to sell.
How will you respond on the off chance that you concoct an extraordinary thought for an advanced sticker?
 Is it conceivable to sell it in the i-Message App Store? It's absolutely impossible.

Likewise, NFTs have an element that you can empower that will pay you a rate each time NFT is sold or moved, guaranteeing that if your work is more famous and have more exorbitant costs, you will receive a portion of the rewards.

I'm a buyer.

One of the most obvious advantages of purchasing art is that it allows you to to help your #1 specialists, and this is likewise valid for NFTs (which are much further developed, similar to Telegram stickers). At the point when you purchase NFT, you frequently get fundamental use rights, for example, having the option to post a picture on the web or customize your profile picture. There are additional rights to flaunt being innovative, upheld by the blockchain section.

No, I intended to be an authority or collector.

Indeed, NFTs can work similarly just like some other theoretical resource by getting it, and ideally, its cost goes up over the long haul so you can sell it at a benefit. Notwithstanding, I feel messy about bringing it.

Things being what they are, is each NFT unique?

All NFT is a one-of-a-kind image in the blockchain in an exhausting, specialized sense. Nonetheless, it might appear as though a van Gogh's drawing, with just a single form, or it might appear as though an exchanging card, with 50 duplicates or many duplicates with similar drawing numbers.

Who can pay a huge number of dollars for something that is an exchanging card?

That, to some extent, makes the NFTs less compelling. A few groups treat them as the fate of gathering compelling artwork (read: as a jungle gym for the exceptionally rich), while others treat them as Pokémon cards (open to everybody yet in addition a jungle gym for the rich). Logan Paul as of late sell some of the NFTs identified with the $ 1 million Pokémon card box.

Please put an end to it. This is going in a direction that I despise.

Yes, sell NFT video cuts for up to a maximum margin of $ 20,000, which are simply portions from the video you can watch on YouTube at whatever point you need. He likewise sold Logan Paul Pokémon cards as NFTs.

Who can pay $ 20,000 for a Logan Paul video cut ?!

I think a simpleton with his cash is immediately partitioned?

On the off chance that Logan Paul chooses to sell another 50 NFTs for a similar video, it will be silly.

Mike Shinoda of Linkin Park (who additionally sold some NFTs for the melody) is really saying. It is totally unthinkable for an individual to do as such if he somehow managed to turn into a "debased slanted man," as he puts it. I'm not saying Logan Paul is that way; I'm trying to say you must be cautious about who you purchase from.

Full. Indeed, would I be able to purchase human teeth like NFT?

Further endeavors have been made to interface NFTs to certifiable articles, frequently as a method for the check. Nike has the patent to utilize the NFT framework to check the realness of tennis shoes, called Crypto-Kicks. However, no, I haven't got additional teeth at this point. I'm frightened to look.

Look? Where right?

Numerous business sectors have jumped up to the margin of NFTs, permitting individuals to purchase and sell them. The decisions of OpenSea, the other one is Raible, and the last one is Grimes, the Nifty Gateway, are among them, however, there are some more.

There were felines required, as per what I heard. If it's not too much trouble, tell, what's, the account of the huge doggies.....

While the Ethereum containing the blockchain added for the support of NFTs as a feature of another norm, they got as innovatively proficient as could be expected. All things considered, a game called CryptoKitties, which permits clients to sell and sell visual felines, was one of the primary plans. Web, much obliged.

I love kittens.
Not nearly it' depends on the buyer who paid $170,000 for single only.

Arrr

Essentially, the chicks show that a fascinating aspect regarding NFTs (for those of us who are not keen on building an advanced winged serpent workmanship scene) is the means by which they can be utilized in games. NFTs are as of now accessible as items in certain games. NFTs can be utilized to sell land plots. Players can purchase a game weapon, a head protector, or anything like NFT, which can be adaptable for individuals to appreciate.

Would I be able to eliminate the historical center heist to take NFTs?

That is opposing. Part of the blockchain fascination is that it keeps all exchanges, making it harder to take and exchange than rather, a historical center work of art. Notwithstanding, digital currencies have been assigned previously, so everything relies upon how NFT is kept up and how much exertion the casualty might place in to get their cash back.

Note: Don't need to steal! Please
Should I be concerned that digital art will still exist in 500 years?
Most likely. Real my include bit rod: image quality degrades, file formats become unreadable, websites go down, and people forget their wallet passwords. Physical art in museums, on the other hand, is shockingly fragile.

I want to make the most of my blockchain experience. Is it possible to buy NFTs with cryptocurrencies?
Yes, indeed. Most likely. Ethereum is accepted by a large number of marketplaces. However, it's very important to sell NFTs technically and any currency you can demand!

Will NFTs add to global warming and cause Greenland to melt?
It's something to keep an eye out for. NFTs consume much power consumption, because they can by utilize the same method of technology as energy-intensive crypto-currencies. People are working to address this problem, but many of NFTs are still in linked to the Crypto, that are the main source of greenhouse gases elimination. After learning about the potential effects of NFTs on climate change, a few artists have decided not to sell them or have canceled future drops. I am very thankful to the one of my, coworkers has done a thorough investigation, so that you can to find guidance, so only read this complete picture.

NFTs are dump in wallets that are known as digital wallets, just like crypto-currencies. However, you could always store a wallet holding may be on a computer in a bunker underground.

The Opportunities with NFTs

Potential Benefits when you can imagine the art's resale value, NFTs are now very compelling opportunity in market. It's similar to purchasing physical works of art. If you only intend to keep the art, having possession of it will not bring you any benefits. Of course, staring at that work of art may provide you with a sense of fulfillment. Big money, however, comes from selling that piece of art to the highest bidder. To put it another way, if you can buy a one-of-a-kind NFT and then sell it for more than you paid for it, you could profit handsomely.

The perfection of blockchain is that it eliminates the possibility of fraud and theft. There will be codes and authentication to verify and verify the authenticity of the work of art you own. Others can still make copies of an original piece of digital art, but only one original exists. The original belongs to the person who owns the NFT for that piece of art.

Are NFT Stocks The Right Investment For You?

When someone asked you in January what NFT stocks were, you'd probably look at them blankly. As I previously stated, many of them have nothing to do with which the containing the NFTs. However, based on speculation, investors believe these companies will gain exposure to NFTs.

It's difficult to say whether NFT stocks will take off in the long run at this point. Examine cannabis stocks and crypto-currencies from

2017 to 2019. If history is any guide, the hype surrounding NFT stocks will likely fade away soon. With all of the hype, it's easy to dismiss it as science fiction that will never come to pass. However, if we look closely, we are imagine that there is something is going on behind the scenes. And why am I saying this? Last year, according to Nonfungible.com, the total value of NFT transactions increased to $250 million. NFT transactions totaled more than $220 million in the last month alone. It appears that we are witnessing something that is growing at an exponential rate.

CHAPTER TWO

Will NFTs Be the Future of Modern Art?

Traditionally, any digital art that is shared, saved, or downloaded on the internet can be easily shared, saved, and downloaded. However, because anyone can use it, there isn't a strong sense of ownership. Assume you're an artist, a particularly talented one. You also produce some of the most stunning works of art. But what about putting your creativity to good use? You appear to have had no luck with it thus far, at least with the majority of people. However, there is a way to give digital art a sense of individuality using NFTs. It also provides an incentive for good artists to continue producing creative works.

The art industry has a lot of potential for NFTs. However, first and foremost, the market must be regulated. There is currently no rule dictating who is allowed to create NFTs and who is not. Until then, I wouldn't invest in NFT stocks without first waiting for the dust to settle. But, don't get me wrong: I appreciate art. I truly believe that this has the potential to change the way art is viewed in our society. I think that it may be I, but before investing in NFT stocks, I'd want who concrete is developing. However, this is merely my opinion; the final decision is yours to make. Make sure you do your homework and research.

How NFTs Are Shaking Up the Art World?

Big Bang NFT Collectors and Speculators have spent more than $200 million on various kinds of NFT-based collectibles over the course of the year, according to market research firm NonFung.com. Before this, a creative digital artist named Beeple sold a piece for a record-setting $69 million at Christie's on March 11th.

Copyright protection claims are best understood as computer files combined with verification of ownership, such as a registration paper. They exist on a tamper-proof public ledger, like Bitcoin. Similar to dollars, each cryptocurrency is fiat, i.e., each BTC is the same as any other currency. Unlike NFTs, a Rembrandt or a Picasso's paintings don't have any particular value assigned to them, which can be different from buyer to the buyer; the set value of each painting is determined by the highest bidder. To successfully sell their work in an online virtual asset platform, artists will have to sign up and then 'mint'submit' their details on a blockchain (typically the Ethereum blockchain, a rival platform to Bitcoin). Usually, the answer to your question is between $40 and $200. They can then place their ad on an NFT eBay.

Regardless of their monetary value, the whole project seems ludicrous: wealthy collectors offering six to eight figures for works that can typically be obtained for free. Critics have characterized the NFT phenomenon as nothing more than a market mania, a pun on "this year's digital game retailer crash," as the recent boom-and-and-bust experience around GameStop stocks. It is attracting a disparate mixture of artists and speculators who desire to cash in on the latest fad.

It might be a bubble. But today's digital artists, who have been consistently overpromising and underdelivering for years on platforms like Facebook and Instagram, have chosen to seek their fortune elsewhere. Artists—authors, musicians, and filmmakers alike—see a changed world in which there is now a practical ability to "own" and "sell" ability" of digital objects. Artists of all ages and abilities will be given opportunities to meet, connect, and gain a new career path. They put many hours and soul into their work as an artist." If it makes them feel good to be rewarded on an appropriate scale, it is pleasant. Futures could play a central role in achieving the blockchain revolution long-as-as-promised revolution that has major ramifications for mortgages, health care, and personal data management.

Because it's available at no cost, digital art has long been undervalued. The contribution of scarcity is crucial for artists in creating financial value for their work. For some collectors, it is much more important to possess the original item. Few will pay that much money for cardboard with a picture of Honus Wagner, a legendary Pirate, because of scarcity. Additionally, sneakerheads love involves getting the latest releases from Nike and Adidas, as Martin is said to have bought the sole Wu-Tang Clan album for $2 million two years ago.

It's easier to understand the fact that baseball cards, sneakers, and a Wu-Tang Clan CD can be valuable when you can see and touch them, but a food CD in a restaurant, a watch in a waiting room, and a bag of heroin aren't. It is also more difficult to see the significance of the creative or digital media since it is easily transmittable."

On the other hand, many digital artists claim that they're paying in part for labor as well as for the images. They want the digital artwork to be considered an emerging media form. Eager to discover her passion, she explores the creative possibilities of drawing, who said, "I want you to be able to look at these items and see that they are all unique." We had good value for our investment in the product because the artist had put so much time and effort into it. Now that most of us have spent most of the year in cyberspace, it's becoming increasingly clear to us what the alternative lifestyle is all about. If you spend nearly all your time in the virtual world, it makes sense to use the money on virtual items.

The digital art era started in 2017 with the release of Crypto-Kit. Most fans have spent over $32 million in one way or another acquiring, trading, and breeding one-anime-style cartoon cats with widgeon eyes. Fortnight players spent an average of $82 in-real-84 dollars on content each year this year. At the same time, crypto currency values have soared; tech celebrities like Elon Musk and Mark Cuban have made significant investments. The sudden rise in the value of Bitcoin and other crypto currencies in 2017, for instance, such as digital collectibles or non-fungible tokens, show just how low in mania this particular area is.

When they saw an opportunity, technology entrepreneurs Duncan and Griffin Foster started a platform called Nifty Gateways last March. At the time, NFT (New Form of Technology) art was just becoming popular, but no one wanted to give or sell work with anything new. Ease of use and accessibility gave Nifty an incentive for wider adoption. The project was in such an early stage, and we had no hopes for success. Due to its wide-reaching appeal, it appealed to a lot of Net-savvy Gallery customers, who were happy to buy and sell $100 million in artwork in the first year. OpenSea and MPlace saw a similar rise in their usage; they normally make up to 15% of their sales in the first month or two.

More and more people and more businesses and celebrities are getting into the act NBA official app Top Shot has sold over $390 million in NFT packages since its October release, trade on the digital trading card platform run by Dapper Labs, according to the NBA. Gronk, a gridiron superstar, sold over a million trading cards of his Super Bowl touchdown highlights, and the Kings of Leon netted over $2 million after selling only two CDs. The Twitter founder was reportedly asked to reveal his first-ever tweet, and it is expected to go for at least $2.5 million dollars at auction. It has been an orgy of activity in the past few months, with high-energy dramas playing out almost daily. Perhaps one of his more understated revelations was this: "I'm pretty f*cked right now," he quipped after breaking his record for-the-all-time sale.

He believes that so-called whales, a.k.a. big whales, are working in the NFT field (financial news trading) world. This, pair of big-money investors and evangelists have a substantial financial interest in anything crypto-related and a great deal to gain from the resultant hype. The Winklevoss brothers invested in Nifty Way in excess of $700,000 into their crypto currency of choice in late 2019 when it was among the top 25 crypto currencies by market capitalization.

Whale Daniel Maegaard, an Australian bitcoin trader, has reportedly made $15 million or more since 2017. More specifically, Maegaw has spent and made back millions in digital art and other NFT-based items, like a virtual property in AxInfinity, with more than $1 million dollars of her $1.5 million investment. Initially, Maera saw

NFT as a means of accumulating wealth-making mechanism, but he's now become a true fan of the work and eagerly posts about new acquisitions and sales. He's particularly fond of one picture called Breaking Bad White, which resembles a pixelated human form," For Maerdy as his social media avatar, he has turned down a million-dollar buyout offer. That reputation is now synonymous with me. What would I be if I ever sold him my services to a company?

But even if an investor regards NFT works as just another investment, he or she is helping artists increase their wallets, too. In psychedelic, glitchy digital video, Andrew Benson has been tinkering with it for years. For the past twenty years, he has had a job as a full-time artist but also has done some commissions like MIIAA and Aphex Twin. I have held this belief for many years: To be successful as an artist, the only option is to not be successful as an artist.

It wasn't going well a year and a half ago when his plans to show new videos to the public failed. He wonders, "Do I have to do all this work, then find locations to display it?" Next, his friend at an NFT Foundation organization requested he submits something. He didn't believe it was very creative, but he included it on the site because he thought that the Internet was a good way to get more traffic. It will produce a Rorsch in a dynamic, kinetic-colored state of mind for $1,250. Since then, he has been able to place a total of 10 pieces in the same price bracket. Now he wonders if he can become self-support anguished. It actually shook my worldview. In this instance, it really takes me back to thinking like an artist; when I see the work I've created, I find a context and a place where it can have an impact.

Noted creative and open-minded contemporary artists are getting their due from NFT collectors as well. Graphics with whirling 3D scenes, saturated color palettes, and witty cartoons abound in today's world. With a younger generation raised on the Instagram app and the masses who have no familiarity with fiat currency, these internet aesthetics are catching the attention of people now- and Twitter-feed customers. Fintech is something for punks. Street art and anti-establishment styles help convey that to others those fintech customers are simply punks in the mainstream.

This is good news for those in the conventional world because they no longer fear for their position in the market. A , New York-based collector. We're at a watershed moment of inflection: the interest and mental energy of the demographic are significantly below that of the beginning of the Internet. Rival auction house Christie demonstrated that even if other powerhouses could not grasp the financial benefit of the artist, Pak understood the music genre.

In the absence of the establishment's support, artists of all ages are engaging in collaborative production in tight-knit NFT-run, single communities, echoing artists from past movements and receiving feedback from each other and generations, and this influences their thinking and approach and output. It's a totally selfless ethos in the digital arts and design space. Mostly in independent music and fine art, there is a belief that the project will fail unless a single person dominates. There's a feeling of everyone being able to benefit from this.

There are cases where the minnows and the whales are migrating together. It turned out to be a personal collecting group in the $69 million, called the Metapurse, two Singaporean investors who were exploring joint venture models built on cutting-edge technology. In January, the two purchased 20 Beeple works of art, cataloged them in a virtual gallery for free, and divvied the business into a collection of 5,400 tokens. These concepts now have six times their value as of March 16th. It is speculated that the team will display their latest headline-making acquisition in a state-of-of-the-the-the-art virtual museum. It is to bring the world of art and creativity to everybody's door.

The market for NFTs, with respect to artists, speculators, and collectors, also has a dark side. With such high entry costs and technical expertise required, some creators might opt out of participating in the action. Many fear that younger artists of color will be marginalized within the "traditionally white" art world. The legal community is focused on the understanding of this new development due to the work of artists being copied and sold without their permission. It's giving people new opportunities to profit from other people's work.

Finally, there are environmental issues to be taken into consideration. There is a considerable amount of computing power used to create NFTs, and many servers run on fossil fuels. Cryptocurrency specialists warn that the "the environmental impact of blockchain's distributed ledger technology is huge," though an adjunct professor of visual arts at New York University is sure of their assessment.

There is less impact on the future of the climate with a new blockchain. For instance, they are finding new uses for NFT technology already. Some people, for instance, pay tokens when their performance is broadcast as a second run, like an actor receiving a royalty check every time their show airs on TV. Music rights management startup Bitmark has rolled out a new model called NFT-like that will let music producers all over the world receive a share of the profits from their artists' works In contrast to companies like Facebook and Instagram, which give non-fans rights and do not allow payment, those who join the NFT online communities receive ownership of the platform and make money in the form of direct compensation.

Many technology evangelists continue to believe that digital currency and blockchain platforms have the ability to change the world in profound ways, so for them, the latest NFT craze is nothing new In Utah, blockchain has already been employed to secure the voting process at Nationwide Insurance, and fight against insurance fraud at Optum Health and others. Advocates say that it could help companies create a transparent supply chain by aggregating knowledge, offer joint aid, and lower financial discrimination in lending.

It has so much to offer to society that we should make an attempt to manage that as much as possible. In the world of new ideas, everything from new product launches to media, and you can see a "idealarming" improvement followed by a "grotesque failure" syndrome. I focus on what is feasible.

Becoming Successful in NFTs Market

what steps you must take in order to be successful in the new media market

In order to find artistic success in NFTs, you may have 02 must ingredients: good judgment and an audience. Unfortunately, artists who dabble in cryptocurrencies and blockchain protocols spend most of their time trying to build their fan base and avoid scammers. Due to the claim that Beeple made that it had appeared overnight, he had actually been developing his digital skills for ten years prior to his first NFT success. Every day consists of a 5,000-day drawing challenge is a culmination of the work he's done over the last 5,000 days to strengthen his practice.

Griffin Cock Foster, the partner in Nifty Gateway, believes that the greatest crypto artists have the most skill. "I believe that being an artist is a set of skills in and of itself," he says. Thinking outside the box necessitates doing something different than anyone else has done before. Successful people are the ones who are technically creative.

Judging the quality of the art is entirely a matter of personal taste. It's almost impossible to command millions of people when you don't have such institutes such as the Christie are backing you. Artsy CEO Mike Steib maintains that the NFT market is not really a free-for-all, to be sure. who was responsible for the sale of Beelzebubber?" For his part, he contends. The biggest gate in the art world, Christie's, was satisfied with the Beeple deal.

"GOOD ART WILL AT TIMES TAKE THE FORM OF AN NFT, BUT THE CONVERSE ISN'T ALWAYS TRUE"

The traditional art market as a whole remains cautious about crypto currency. Stibbe, who works with e-commerce sites developing and hosting galleries of fine art, states that auction headlines drive art price increases even when NFTs are involved. They are at a fraction of the size of sports cards, which are in the ballpark of $8 to $10 billion, according to our research.

Even with regard to items in the world of crypto currency, Steib is uneasy about classifying them as such. He claims that "good" or "fine" art exists in "whenever" There's no better word than 'It's art,' but a Crypto Kitty [fungible creature] is not art, a Crypto Punk [technically proficient]is not art, and a Top Shot [trading card]is a layup in the NBA isn't an NBA player, but it's my be so called one's person opinion.'

He disagrees with Christie's on Beeple's estimation of his current worth, classifying him as another contemporary art superstar in the class of Koons and Hockney. I don't think that Christie's sold one of the rarest and famous Pokémon cards for $1 billion.

EXCESS FIAT CURRENCY, EXCESS CRYPTOCURRENCY

Getting good academic training and joining an artist's cooperative can be necessary for artists to achieve a measure of success in the art world. Work will reward a lifetime of appreciation for those who devote their entire lifetimes to it, Steib tells us.

Underpinning this NFT is not a myth; there are no preconceptions of any kind that drive it," he concludes. The second question is, Can I survive without the support of infrastructure and industry in this size NFT? I think I'm up to the task of following in Beeple's footsteps. To put it mildly, I would say, stay in school, kid.

NFTs aren't a democratizing force in the world of fine art auctions. In an editorial written statement released in March, he estimates that the price MetaKovan, the winner of the Christie's auction, took advantage of the emerging commercial rules of art appreciation and inflated the value of the pieces.

No rational reasons exist to assume that Beeple's elixir can increase 100 times or more in value in the highly volatile and mercurial crypto market. Instead of democratizing the art market, buying in Bitcoin effectively takes it even further into the stratosphere." MetaKovan is a substitute for an elite group that possesses fiat currency.

Defining the Crypto Art Movement

Cock Foster has spoken about the response to NFTs being the result of a lack of understanding.

"If you see other people making and disseminating art, it must be upsetting," he states. It's possible that being a traditional art critic could upset you. I suppose they are not widely accepted as an art movement, in the sense that they are not widely understood.

When asked for a working definition of the crypto movement, he finds it difficult to offer an answer. I believe the movement is still in the process of defining its identity. This is a network of networks." Everyone has their own fan base. I suppose it is very interesting, and something we have never seen before.

THE "MONA LISA OF CRYPTO ART" AND NEW CONNOISSEURS
In the absence of galleries and critics, the people who actually champion the crypto movement are the true champions of art. Design software engineer Dylan Field, the 27-year-year-old founder and CEO of Figma, On March 12, on Clubhouse, Erik spoke about the love he has for CryptoPunk, a form of early ERC-20 NFTs on the

Ethereum network. Zombie-like drawings and AI-like drawings of aliens were produced by Matt Hall and John Watkinson.

While the field serves as a good foil to those who think that NFTs are purchased only for money, these farmers have given them much thought and work, and faith. He completely lost his sense of reality.

Most of ourselves have developed close ties with having our own punks. We saw them as bearers of our hopes and dreams. Let's not discuss them anymore. Sometimes we dream about them even if we don't realize it. The punks permeate our identities—they serve as face covers.

LARVA LABS / DYLAN FIELD / PERUGGIA

During his presentation, the presenter spoke about the value he placed on one particular 10,000 character alien from that batch of 10,000 CryptoP images and described it as "reassuring." He went on to explain that he wanted to raise the status of the thriving alt-coin art market.

As far as I'm concerned, I believe we will see 7804 as the portrait of Lisa, digitally enhanced.

I believe we should make 7804 the patron saint of digital art or maybe an alien because if you insist. For me, it was strange that no one agreed 7804 was the most valuable punk musician. The name bothered me as much as it represented the crypto movement itself. This results in a paradox since it must also change hands for the movement to be viewed as a symbol.

Despite its dissemination is free at first, the field's bid succeeded, and it for $7.5 million in 2018, a connection to the celebrated Art Deco robber Michelangelo Rosselli increased the value of Leonardo da Vinci's painting to $15 million when he purchased it in 2017. He ended his letter with the famous Albert Peruggia's well-known words: "Enjoy your time while you have it. It won't last." But please know that you will put nothing over the finished piece until it is publicly accepted as the most valuable artwork. As a result, you'll be short on your time with it. You'll always wonder why you gave away the digital Mona Lisa once you've parted with it.

SUCCESSES BEYOND BEEPLE

While the protocols and equipment operators are still being finalized, many people in the Beeple area have acquired new skills in the process. He based his Nike-influenced homage, "The Trey of Traps," on René Magritte's work, on a sale in which it fetched approximately $7,200 in the Philippines. He receives just over half the average yearly pay in the Philippines because of one NSFTA.

He transformed his whole life from "troubled childhood" to "like shipwrecked," an 18-year-old Las Vegas sketch artist when he started peddling his artwork on the NFT market. His term of endearment for his private notebook was called "F-Word", was told by the Gotham magazine. Instead of: "It was like, "I'm going to work very hard and be the most successful." Once he'd earned his fair share of money from his work in the crypto and in sneaker endorsements, he could afford to rent an apartment in Seattle on his own. He has made $4 million this month selling NFTs.

Some observers are hopeful that NFTs may end up offering an equitable compensation model for all digital authors.

Now, it's upon when we are discussing the topic of systemic bias and equal chance for all the places which can be around it. Who would object to decentralizing power at the expense of a larger institution?

THE RESALE VALUE OF NFTS

Because an item can be linked to one or reused via NFTs, creators can potentially be compensated for every time it is used or sold, which makes it a piece of work. "The most important thing in NFTs is what happens after the first transaction," Leonard believes.

Leon Leonard thinks Beeple's auction is a historical instance of radical change for everything from videos and typefaces to musical compositions and logos.

I really believe in that , this is the major thing that will affect the worlds of all kinds of artistic endeavors as well as long as it becomes prominent in our awareness. In order to accomplish that, he has realized that they need to come to terms with environmental concerns like mining' He says, "It's a return to the earlier days of the internet,"

CHAPTER THREE

Creating Process involved in NFTs

the" 'Beeple Mania': How Mike Wintmack Gets Millions Selling Pixels" explains the phenomena in question

Why would someone spend $777 on an MP4? Wouldn't you be watching that on Instagram for free?

Theoretically, yes, but crypto art only ensures the authenticity of a single piece of digital art with block chain technology. To comprehend the noticeable price of having such art piece is in New York City, one must be familiar with non-fungible tokens, or digital currency, which is the preferred method for housing that hold an emerging brand website. EXIST. In 2018, Nifty Gateway was founded by Duncan Foster, who is 26 years old, and his identical twin, Griffin. You can think of NFTs as similar to a pair of fancy shoes that cost a lot of money.

And thus: Nifty Gateway—prominent, upstarts that competes with Makers and SuperRare in the sector of digital asset management—assigns an original artwork to a digital asset account and permanently store it in its holdings. Everyone who has Internet access to the web can identify that piece of information.

How to Buy NFTs

Neo is one of many NFT marketplaces: MakersPlace, Nifty Gateway, OpenSea, SuperRare, Rarible, and Decentraland are only a few. When it comes to NBA memorabilia, the collection is over $230 million has already been done through Top Shot—where tokicks for your highlights.

YellowHeart - King of Leon uses a blockchain-aware service to prevent ticket fraud and get tickets more directly into fans' hands. Many argue that it would might be the Future of the music concerts and allows artists to control more of their destiny.

Making & Selling NFTs

Would you say you are creative or just looking to make money? You could interpret your work in any manner you want. A$580,000 worth of Nyan Pop-Tarts can be turned into a cute Pop-Tart animation of Nyan Cat. As a general rule, it is accepted that your cost will differ from one site to another (to cover the "gas" of PCs required available to be purchased on stages like Ethereum). You may likewise discover the venture eliminated from the Nifty Web Site, where it's easy to apply for an NFT application in their market. There are numerous issues when peeling back the initial NFT layers; ethical, logistical, and environmental difficulties arise.

Numerous specialists have featured the overwhelming effect of NFT assignment and exchange on a corrupted planet through environmental change, ecological separation, and natural imbalance.. So, NFTs may have something to do with global warming? To summarize, it can be stated as follows: Creating NFTs by producing them on the blockchain, combined with the high tide of trading (bidding, selling, etc.), will make up a significant amount of overall blockchain use If greed is taken to the nth degree, we could face a new type of environmental destruction. Ethereum, the blockchain which contains many of these NFTs, is planning to implement proof-of-of-stake to lower energy consumption, but the proof-of-of-stake initiative hasn't materialized yet. At this point, it's unclear if there will be a change.

Ethically, the act of selling NFTs may not be quite what it could be. A noted digital artist RJ Palmer has recently issued a warning on Twitter about an account cloning his or her colleagues' art and selling it as authentic works of digital artworks. It is a great opportunity for young artists to see their work exploited without recourse or verification that the issuer is really the author and copyright owner. The anonymity afforded by crypto has made them vulnerable to theft and danger.

What might be best example of Selling NFTs?
It might be a better question to ask what hasn't already been NFT'd. It's no more than the matter of having the hottest names of all join the non-fungible token markets: technology, music, finance, and business. Let's use "zoo animal" as an example: when something works, keep using it: "don't fix it if it ain't broke.

All of the content on this page is pulled in from Twitter." You might be able to locate the same content at a different website, or you might discover additional information, though.

A group of "art lovers and artists" purchased a Bansky, and then used the money to start a new painting. It was offered to purchase on the online marketplace for $50,000. (She was also prologue that, want to proceeds "charities that accept Bitcoin to empower younger generations in order for them to adapt and learn about this revolution that humanity is witnessing.") Rob Gronkowski is currently earning about $1,000,000,000 a card for his limited-edition Championship ring autographs. But mercifully, Elon Musk basically was the originally planned to give a best techno song that was about the NFTs was an album title. It's estimated that a number of Aoki's work "Cat" sketches have brought in over $4.25 million, and a number are still available to purchase at less than $5 million.

What will be the Future of Digital Currencies?

"You may be right, but it is DIGITAL now." Now, it's the word "digital," which comes from the Latin word "digitus," which means "finger, toe," or computers, and music players, wristwatches, cell phones, etc. So, what are you're you saying about digital money and even digital citizenship?

And then came the book press, lauded as a liberator by many. Once upon a time, books were available only to the wealthy. We now have e-books and other devices that anyone can use. Despite being digital and having been converted to words, we still prefer a physical book over a piece of electronic plastic that must be recharged to function. If you truly believe in the proposition that digital currencies such as bitcoin can make positive change in the world, how?

If you want to give the answer of this question, its must important to investigate money in regards to how we conceive of a better 'world for all, and we must ask how we use it, why we do, and include will be in the model. I've learned that money, unlike other forms of property, can be used prior to an occurrence even taking place. There is nothing implied by its innumerable manifestations and effects, yet its only simple meaning is good or bad. It's a special but often misunderstood and underutilized ingredient. This demonstrates the point that money is neutral when used to buy and sell but complex when applied to other purposes such as ethical or moral decision making. Endogenous and exogenous, in the same way, at the same time, since it has characteristics that are intrinsic to its culture while at the same time is dependent on the global community. The device lacks an identity and can be easily replaced, yet it is seen as a non-renewable asset within the broad context. As a matter of principle, however, results are never entirely predictable, and if you want to use it, it may not essential requirement.

A currency must be believed to have inherent value by those who hold it. The U.S. Senate Committee on Homeland Security and the Government concurred in November 2013 that unmistakable monetary forms, like Bitcoin, are a genuine type of revenue. Migrant laborers can utilize the 'Bitcoin organization' to send cash to their families without giving them high charges because of low exchange expenses. A European Commission estimated that if the global fee for remittance is lowered to 5% (which the G20 backed in 2011), an additional US$15 billion could be supplied to developing countries. These money transfer services could be disinter mediated through an infrastructure-based system.

Crypto currencies are unique in that they are both distributed and decentralized. Because of the Internet, we may be only seeing the 'tip of the iceberg' discoveries of new applications that will give rise to undiscovered marketplaces. To function more efficiently, in the past, the corporation had to entrust control to a large number of people; today, the dependency on a network has opened the door to the "ability" network's power" up to a small number of elites with dominant interests. It has been said that Bitcoin is money's move to decentralization, and it may be considered to be a more streamlined system approach. Bitcoin represents a paradigm shift equal to file sharing peer-to-to-peer and telephony (Skype, for example).

Almost no regulations have been established for digital or virtual currencies, but existing laws can differ greatly according to each jurisdiction's financial regulations: taxation, stock, securities, criminal, or civil rights, pensions, commodities, or social security, consumer protections, etc. The two primary problems that, bitcoin faces are whether it is legal tender and whether it is an asset. There are a number of currencies in the world that are expressly made the money of another country (e.g., US dollars, which the government recognizes). Germany allows the usage of units of a priori of account that are commonly regarded as private money as a world leader in the effort to reduce transaction costs. Under the first scenario, the obvious disparity is that, unlike tangible property, digital currencies, digital currencies have the capacity to be divided into many small parts, albeit briefly, which is not immediately obvious. When a country's economy is developed, that generally means it has made it inordinately easier for digital currencies to thrive. In truth, there has been an extraordinary amount of guidance provided by the USA, and that can be seen below. Capital-controlled economies are implicitly antagonistic because they can effectively be defined as having control of their money supply. African and a few other countries' concerns have not in the state that they will be further considered?

It is evident that the value of bitcoin cannot be realized through democracy since it is subject to market forces, and this can impact our social objectives. However, any new crypto-currency could possibly implement more egalitarian monetary policies, financial and governance models.

So what if a "digital currency" could make a real contribution to those social issues, e.g., inclusive culture, equal opportunity, or mutualism; wouldn't those be positive contributions?" With the rise of virtual currencies, such as bitcoin, the pace of innovation in the crypto-currency space has picked up.

These factors influence the effectiveness of money in bringing about social and environmental change, whether it be through political ideology, the economic environment, community aspiration, or individual desire. In cases where a local currency could be created to build a more resilient local economy and enhance socioeconomic well-being, an investigation into a national currency must be undertaken. When the current economic system falters, one can see such symptoms as an increase in social divisions, higher crime, decreased physical well-being, low social participation, and an absence of a sense of community.

CHAPTER FOUR

Block chain - for Normal People

Traditionally, a transaction requires an intermediary to act as a go-between. Assuming that Rob wants to transfer $20 to Melanie, let's assume that he would have to give her $10 worth of bitcoin. He can either give her £20 in cash or transfer it to her account via an app of his choice. In both cases, a bank is an institution that verifies a transaction: One is with a physical withdrawal, the other is with an app. It is up to the bank to decide whether the transaction is done. The bank updates all transactions pertaining to Rob whenever he pays or receives money. or in other words, the ledger is held and controlled by the bank.

Without being completely confident in his banker, Rob would not risk his money. He needs to feel confident that the bank will not take advantage of him, or that he'll lose his money, that he won't be robbed, and that it won't disappear without warning tomorrow morning. Even in the financial crisis of 2008, when banks were proven to be irresponsible, the government preferred to rescue them and risk the total destruction of trust.

Another thing about blockchains is that is essential to know is that they are entirely decentralized. There is no central authority like a bank, there are no deposit boxes, and balances are distributed across all participants. Rather, each node stores a complete ledger is on its own hard drive. Nodes on the network that have the same ledger are connected by software known as a peer-to-to-peer (P2P) client, which ensures everyone has the latest version of the ledger at any given time.

State-of-of-the-the-the-the-art cryptographic technology is used to encode each new transaction as it is entered. Once the transaction is encrypted, it is known as a block, and it's equivalent to a collection of various transactions. That block is then sent throughout the computer network of nodes, where it is verified, and once verified, added to the previous list of blocks. The 'chain' is known as a large

network of multiple, linked computers, and therefore the tech is called a 'blockchain' by default.
Once the transaction has been recorded in the system, it can be finished. Basically, this is how cryptocurrency transactions like Bitcoin work.

Accountability and the removal of trust
This system has many advantages over banking or a central clearing system, doesn't it? It seems unlikely that Rob would use normal currency instead, doesn't it?
Let's put it this as simply as we can: "The answer is trust." Rob must know that his bank will protect his money and safeguard it because of the nature of his business. Additionally, large regulatory systems are created to ensure that banks are working efficiently. If you want something done right, do it yourself. The role of the Financial Services Authority is to prevent this type of mess from happening in the first place. Many banks have made many mistakes in the past, but we have also seen this time and time and time again. Power can easily be abused when you have a single source of authority. The trust between people and financial institutions is uncertain and tenuous: we distrust each other, but not one another.
Blockchain systems, however, require you to have zero faith in them. All transactions (or blocks) must be verified by the network, and committed to the ledger is a single point of failure, and an open record of each transaction process is shared by all nodes. To hack the ledger on a blockchain, an attacker would have to take control of hundreds of thousands of nodes at the same time, an exceptionally difficult task. A system or network hacker would also need to be able to shut down all the computer systems distributed across the world.
One factor that must be considered in creating security is the encryption process itself. Decentralized verification processes like the Bitcoin's are purposefully designed to make it difficult to tamper with. Verification is avoided in the case of Bitcoin because of the processor- and time-intensive calculations required, such as puzzles or complex mathematical formulas. Completing the resource validation process gets you some Bitcoins and a transaction fee. People will be motivated to join the network, as there is a strong requirement for fast and capable computers as well as electricity in order to run this, and money will be made. This is called "mining" because it requires a lot of effort (for the machine, in this case). In addition, transactions are verified as independent as far as possible in the hands of the government.

This decentralization, democratic, and highly secure nature of blockchains mean that they can operate without any government intervention (they're self-regulating), but because of it, they're also unregulated (unregulated), participatory, and mysterious (decentral and clever). Work that, will be in the spite of fact having reason that people do not trust each other.

Wait includes the reasoning that you must understand, and you may have sense of being excited about blockchain will begin to set in.

Smart contracts
From my perspective things, what really makes this interesting is where it can be applied beyond altcoins like Bitcoin. Because of the secure, unmediated transactions being a fundamental concept to the blockchain, it's straightforward to see other ways in which this approach can be advantageous. The more surprising thing is that such applications already exist or are in development. The difference between not getting something done and getting it done right is purely a matter of attention to detail.

It is highly likely that the most exciting things about Ethereum blockchain applications will be smart contracts, which require code to be run to ensure the contract is fulfilled. In simple terms, the code can be used to build a kind of escrow system, as long as the computing system can be made to execute it. As an example, you could create a contract that verifies that a new website has been started. We've done invoicing and chasing - for a long time, and now it's time to innovate. Smart contracts can be used to demonstrate property or artwork ownership. There is a huge reduction in fraud potential here.

Cloud storage (Storj) revolutionized the web, which made the advent of Big Data possible. Most online applications are installed in single-server-based data centers (Amazon, Rackspace, Google, etc.). Like banking, this has the same single-point-of-of-failure problem. Distributed data removes trust completely and will also promise to increase network stability.

The biggest problems we face today are identity theft and data security. The threat to our personal data contained in vast databases run-of-of-the-the-the-mill online services such as Facebook is now enormous For secure data sharing, and the blockchain concept offers a solution by storing your private keys inside encrypted blocks which are verified whenever you need to prove your identity. This can be used in various ways, from the simple replacement of passports to complicated electronic identity cards. We'll go a long

way in contributing to other areas, such as re-configuring passwords. It could be a huge undertaking.
Since Russia's influence on the recent U.S. presidential election was uncovered, digital voting has long been considered both invalid and at risk of manipulation. Anonymity can be preserved while voting on a blockchain platform is offered. One of the promises it makes is that it won't only reduce fraud in elections but also increase participation.

Most of the blockchain's applications are still in the early stages of development. Bitcoin, the most mature blockchain platform, still suffers from extreme volatility, even though it has existed for several years now. The greatest virtue of blockchain is that it has the potential to address the major issues we face today but also makes it an enticing one to pursue. You can rest assured that I'll be keeping an eye on this project.

Steganography in Principle

The oldest form of communication is hiding things in writing, yet it is one of the least-research... Academic curiosity has always been my motivating factor in doing steganography. Although it is only employed in both military and commercial networks, steganography has not received much attention until recently.
The word steganography originates for the Greek word, which translates to "to hide writing." or "to write in a secret code." Krypto means something that is no visible or simply that is hidden, and traces back to the become Greek Word kryptētērion. It was derived from the Greek word graph, which means "to write." A cipher is a goal of writing down something so that even if someone sees it, they can't understand it. All the written form of communication known as steganography, which was popular at one time, is still in use today, but much more rarely now (concealed writing). Stego means hidden. Stego is a way of writing rather than a replacement for cryptography. Although cryptography is part of it, steganography is different. As opposed to plaintext, the goal of cryptography is to obscure the message, and steganography is to hide the fact that one is sending a message. Combining these two techniques enables the embedded secret message to be encrypted first. If people can't detect

the transmission of encrypted messages, they're less likely to find out how important they are.

Hackers and investigators may be attracted to a data field even if it is encrypted and hidden by encrypting it, but they will not make an attempt to obtain the key to gain access. Disguising, data in the least significant bits of the medium while keeping it safe employs steganography. Embedding is necessary that the carrier media retains its color, consistency, appearance, and luster after curing.

Other similar techniques include steganography, which aims to mark an image or sound file so that no one can discover who has altered it, and encumbering, in which modifying the file is an integral part of the process. Makeable alterations should be subtle; no one should be able to overwrite an existing mark or add a new one. This is an exciting new technology for the entertainment industry because it provides a simple method to know if something has been stolen from the web or obtained legitimately.

The Kerckhoff principle applies in steganography as well: An effective steganography system should require the enemy to make an unguessable key choice, rather than knowing how to crack the security.

1.1 Background

Concurrent innovations in information protection and in recent years have focused on the use of hiding rather than on encryption. There were copyright protection and state surveillance. It's inversely proportional to the amount of information on the Internet and public media: the more we put out there, the more we need to protect ourselves from information theft and abuse. Because digital copying is so simple, the music and video industries are particularly concerned Advances in technology should be seen as a boost rather than a threat. Music and video prices and systems; a measure of the problem is the sales may need to be affected; another cause of the problem is copyright protection; one is the music and video pricing, and there are people who object (hiding notices and serial numbers in a way that would be difficult for pirates to remove). Modern methods and systems that can uncover previously unseen information will be extremely useful in digital investigation and digital traffic analysis. Limitations of the current approaches can be taken into account in the design of better methods. The main objective is to keep secrets or prevent other people from keeping secrets.

Reasons Why You Should Buy Paintings Directly From Artists

There are a number of facts supporting the idea that you should not only buy original art in brick-and-and-mortar galleries but have your walls decorated with original paintings and works from well-known artists instead.
That's entirely your own, which is something that no one else has created
Every scene, color, and texture in the painting has been carefully developed.
The item is made of high-quality materials,
There is nothing like it (you get the most value for your buck) in an online or physical gallery.
When you want to add new work to your collection, the price goes up.
Contact the artist and be sure to ask any questions you have.

You get an original unique painting
When you buy an original, hand-handled, original artwork from an artist, you have one of a kind.
There's no danger that your friends, family, or neighbors already have the same painting because your painting can be completely customized with your unique style.

The definition of "original" is "a basis for a copy."
Keep in mind that many sellers who will describe paintings as 'of an original nature can be offering reproductions.
Copies are typically produced in China and Eastern countries at graphic art factories. The workers' working conditions are never ideal. Employees work many hours every day without certain breaks and the production is managed to make in buildings that lack basic needs like glass in window and heating during winter.

There are two mass factories of Danish artists, one located in Copenhagen and the other in Aarhus, which use pseudonyms.

It's difficult to tell whether the painting is an original or a reproduction –the major things that must be consider are the:

The best way to research an artist is to type their name into Google and then take a look at the results. Is the artist's contact information listed? Does his or her website appear?

There are an artist profile and a biography on the website.

If an image of the artist is included, and they have a personal statement
It has many non-replica touches, such as the vibrant colors, like the real paintings, which convey that it is an original work of art.

If he or she is truly creative, there must be an actual creator.
When signed on the back of the canvas, with the full name, title, and year.

The painting is created with great care.
The unique artwork, of true artists develops hours and blending of texture, tone, and color. It results in a piece of art no matter how much work you put into it. You are the only one who will know the depth and texture of your vision as you put more and more and more effort into it.
In the beginning, the artist chose the topic, approach, and medium. When one finishes preparing the canvas for painting, one must prime it, apply texture, paint the subject, and finally coat it with a layer of paint.
It varies a lot, but artists typically work on a painting 5-10 times before it is exhibited in public. Since multiple transparent and translucent layers are needed for the creation of the image, the painting process must be repeated many times.
The characteristic of the reproduction process is that there is a short time allowance of time for making each piece.
This basically means that if the painting is completely dry, you may only paint up to three layers at a time. It will usually be made in one step, and the artist will be working on 50 exact duplicates of it. Because of this, originality is often absent.

You get a quality product.
Many artists are passionate about the quality of their materials and painting, as well as their techniques.
Generally, you can distinguish three types of artist paint: school paint, student paint, and art paint suitable for artists.
The quality of the painting is determined by a number of factors, for instance, the type of paint used, the colors, the way it is applied, the

number of coats, and the brushes used, as well as the painting techniques Whether you use different pigments or just pigments in different amounts, it's a question of which binders are used and the proportions.

Paint is the highest quality when the most expensive pigments are used with the least amount of pigments.
Training quality is the most affordable and is found in the schools. On account of its low quality, it's more suited to home decorating than to avoid interference with other paint and color since it has difficulty with mixing, stays thin and flaky, and does not retain its luster, opacity, tints well, and is low in color strength and transparency.
Good student quality is the foundation paint for painting, which can be used for priming and finish coatings. It has a good sound quality so that colors are mixed within certain limitations. Transparency only seems to be a problem with these shades.
Premium creative quality combines high light fastness, strong coloration, high opaqueness, and translucency. In all, it is an excellent tool for painting both fine details and brilliant colors, as well as for the creation of lifelike paintings. As a result, the paints will be stable, and paintings created with them will retain their brilliance over time.

Many artists prefer to use a high-quality canvas made of cotton or linen.
Varnish or gel is almost always the final protective finish for artists. The use of nontoxic dyes extends the life of the paint and makes it more pleasant to live with."
Forgeries usually use student quality and low-quality paint because that is more affordable. Professional artist paint is seldom used because of its cost. Clones don't get UV and sunlight protection for several years.
They are often made of 100% polyester fabric, which has a surface that does not stretch or deform in relation to the paint's moisture levels.

For every dollar you spend, you get the greatest possible return on investment.
They often pay 50% of the sale price of their artwork, whether they sell it through a physical gallery or online.
When you deal with the artist, there are no third parties to monetize the work, so there are no profits to go around.

YOU GET THE MOST BANGS FOR YOUR BUCK.
In addition, in physical stores and online, you pay more for paintings than you would if you were just starting out as a reseller of an artist.
Generally, you may be able to get 25% of the purchase price that you originally paid for an original piece, whereas custom paintings fall dramatically in price.

If you encounter an artist with ability, you can capitalize on it.
It will require a lot of practice, and knowing what to look for when purchasing artwork is a prerequisite.

You get a better service.
When you are dealing with a person who is an accomplished professional artist, he or she will provide answers. How you build it, how you finish it, how you maintain it, or how you address it is all-important.
There is, of course, the chance that you can end up with an original piece made just by allowing the artist to paint with your own colors and designs.

Many artists help with travel arrangements.

Seven Easy Tips for Selling Your Art

1.) Paint what the buyer desires. Many musicians, as you may know, understand this concept. They sing or play the music that the audience enjoys. Don't get me wrong, her painting skills are fantastic, but no gallery cares if your painting skills are fantastic if they drive people away rather than attracting them to the paintings. People want to feel good, especially in these difficult economic times. That's all there is to it. That is why movies are so popular; people want to escape their daily lives. So, once more, paint what they desire and what sells.
2.) Sell where there are buyers. This is something you hear a lot in real estate. It's all about the location, location, location. The same is true when it comes to selling art. My point is that if you want to sell

any of your work, you need to place it in places where people buy art. So, where are they, you might ask? Identify art galleries, art shows, art festivals, and trade shows that are relevant to your niche. A Fish and Boat Show is a great place to sell work if you paint fish and lours.

3.) Carefully Present Your Artwork: Any successful businessperson understands the importance of maintaining a professional appearance. Cleanliness and neatness are required in the artwork. It's time to tighten the hooks and screws. The display area and tent should be welcoming. Clothes must be clean and in good condition. Also, please refrain from using your cell phone while attending an art show, gallery, or trade show.

4.) Make yourself likable. When dealing with a customer, be courteous. When speaking with potential customers over the phone, always address them by their first name. This will demonstrate to them that you are interested in them. The customer is the most important person. Make sure you pay your bills on time. It would be embarrassing if you lost sales because you didn't pay your cell phone bill or lost your website's host because you didn't pay your cell phone bill. Little things like that can have a long-term negative impact.

5. Make a statement about yourself as an artist. Many art galleries and shows require an artist bio, which is a brief description of yourself and your work.

6.) Have faith in yourself as an artist. There are several artists who, once again, can paint their butts off but refuse to use their skills to supplement their income. They come up with a variety of reasons why they won't be able to set up at the next local art festival. "Oh, I need to buy a tent," "I'm not sure if my work will sell," or "I'm not as good as you" are all examples of excuses. The latter is the one I despise the most. There are people who are truly awful, and there are people who believe my work is terrible, but guess what? My work allows me to earn a living. Fear is major source of the all these excuses. As an artist, you must keep moving forward.

7.) Don't give up. Unfortunately, you will face obstacles and challenges along the way, but the best solution is to dust yourself off and keep moving forward.

How to Start Selling Art

When you're first starting out, selling art can be difficult, and this is true for both online and offline sales. There are numerous theories, methods, and processes that can assist you in selling your artwork, and each will work differently depending on how you work, which areas you are comfortable working in, and how determined you are to sell your work.

Building an Audience
When considering how to sell artwork, this is a factor that is frequently overlooked or assumed to be obvious or common knowledge. There's a slim chance you'll sell anything if you don't have an audience for your work. There are few opportunities for people to see your artwork, talk to you about it, or even buy it if you don't have a good, strong audience, both online and offline.

How do you begin the process of building an audience for your artwork if building an audience is essential to being able to sell it?

Art Fairs
Local art fairs and affordable art fairs may appear intimidating, but they are increasingly becoming democratic platforms for artists to participate in and show their work to a wide audience of art lovers. You can apply for a stand to display your work for the duration of the fair as an individual or as part of an artist collective. You have a good chance of being accepted to the right kinds of art fairs if you submit a well-prepared application.

While art fairs are beneficial in terms of exposing your work to new people and beginning to familiarize an art-hungry audience with your work, there is a cost disadvantage. Acceptance to an art fair usually comes at a cost, which is determined by the size of the stand you want and the amount of exposure you want to gain in things like the fair catalog. Then there's the matter of making your work stand out from the rest of the crowd at the fair.

Don't be put off, though. The advantages of exhibiting your work at an art fair can easily outweigh the costs. Simply plan your mini-exhibition there and arrive with marketing materials such as business cards, flyers, and possibly even brochures of your work that people can take with them.

Exhibition Opportunities

Aside from art fairs, you may be able to take advantage of other exhibition opportunities at local galleries in your area, or you can host your own exhibitions.

Hosting your own exhibition or an exhibition with other local artists can be both fun and beneficial if you have space or the means to rent a commercial space for a short period of time. The chance to show your work to the local holding community can be said as the great gain exposure, and by hosting your own exhibition, you retain a lot of control over how your work is displayed and priced, as such as the 100% of any sales profits.

If you don't feel comfortable hosting your own show, you can apply to local galleries to have your work shown for you. Because you won't be renting the space, this is likely to be far more cost-effective for you; however, you will lose control over sale prices, and the gallery will take between 30 and 50% of the profits from the sale of your work. Having said that, hopefully, the right gallery will properly promote your work and expose you to the right people.

Social Media for Artists

Regardless of one's feelings or opinions about social media, it is undeniably a useful tool for building an audience for artists. Facebook and Twitter, for example, can be great places to build a network of appreciative fans as well as a supportive network.

You can create a profile or page for yourself as an artist on Face book or Twitter, where you can upload pictures of your work and keep people up to date on what you're up to or where you're showing your work offline. You can also join groups and other pages, as well as follow people who are of interest to you. In exchange, you will gain a following of your own.

You should include a link to your own artist website in your profile so that people can see your work in a more private setting.

Build an Artist Website using Art Gallery Website Templates

It may appear difficult to create an artist website, but this should not be the case. There are many services out there that allow you to go to their website, fill in a few details, click a few buttons, and have your very own artist website in minutes. As a result, creating an artist website is a relatively simple task that will pay off handsomely when it comes to building an audience and, eventually, selling your art online.

Having an artist website provides you with a platform for displaying all of your artwork in a centralized hub that you control, organize, and is specifically for your artwork. Of course, there are a plethora of websites that allow you to share your artwork with a large audience, but much like art fairs, this means you'll have to put in a lot more effort to stand out.

Your name and artwork are available to a global audience 24 hrs. available and 07 days a week. when you have your own website. You should be able to have pages of content about yourself and your work in addition to displaying your work. You should also be able to advertise events that you will be attending or exhibitions that you will be having. All of this promotional value is usually available at a very low cost, and the benefits far outweigh the costs.

Promoting Your Website

You should promote your website in everything you do as an important tool for building an audience and developing a following from which you can sell your artwork. Any online profiles you have should include links to your website, and any printed material you create should include your web address.

CHAPTER FIVE

What Are Crypto Assets?

There are thousands of different types of crypto assets – or cryptocurrencies, as you may know, them. You've probably heard of a few of them: Bitcoin, Ripple, Litecoin, and Ethereum have all recently made headlines. But what is it, exactly?

Let's start by dissecting the term "cryptocurrency." The word 'crypto' means 'hidden' or 'secret,' reflecting the security technology used to track who owns what and make payments between users.

The second half of the word, 'currency,' explains why cryptocurrencies were created in the first place: they are a form of electronic cash.

Cryptocurrencies, are not always same as that of the cash we use. They are electronic and operate on a peer-to-peer basis. There is no central bank or government to oversee the system or intervene if it fails.

Some people find this appealing because they believe it gives them more control over their money, but there are significant risks involved. If your funds are stolen, no one is responsible for helping you get your money back because there are no banks or central authorities to protect you.

WHAT CAN YOU BUY WITH CRYPTOCURRENCY?

To put it another way, you wouldn't pay for groceries with cryptocurrency. No major high-street retailer in the United Kingdom accepts cryptocurrency as payment.

Paying with cryptocurrency is generally slower and more expensive than paying with a recognized currency like sterling.

Cryptocurrency is being developed to make it easier to use, but it is still not very money-like at the moment. This is why they are now referred to as "cryptoassets" rather than "cryptocurrencies" by central banks.

Cryptocurrencies are now commonly held as investments by those who anticipate a rise in their value.

While the value of some cryptocurrencies has increased, the value of many others has decreased significantly. They are extremely unpredictable, as shown in the graph below. Even when compared to other volatile assets like oil.

Bitcoin was the only crypto asset available more than a decade ago. The definition has shifted after all these years. You must distinguish crypto assets from cryptocurrencies and digital assets in order to comprehend them.

Meaning Of Crypto Asset

Cryptocurrency and crypto-assets have the same meaning in accounting terms. It can be in the form of a cryptographic asset or a cryptographic currency. Whatever side you choose, keep in mind that these are the computerized assts, not that which are physical ones.. They are assets on the balance sheet in crypto-asset accounting.

What Are Assets in Accounting?

On the sheets, that are the, assets are one the other hand of the liability. They are a company's assets that can be use as tangible or may be not tangible. To have an accurate balance sheet, the total assets must equal the total liabilities and equity. It's also important to understand the difference between fixed and current assets. Inventory is an example of a tangible asset that can be measured and is real. Intangible assets, on the other hand, such as stocks and bonds, are digital.

CRYPTO ASSETS OVERVIEW

There are many different types of crypto assets available on the market. Cryptocurrencies, such as Litecoin, Ripple, Bitcoin, and Ethereum, are examples. To access digital assets using cryptographic techniques, you'll need to use cryptographic techniques. For all financial transactions, it will be used as server medium between the exchange environment.

Utility coins, security coins, and cryptocurrencies are some of the other types of crypto assets. To create more units and transfer assets, the currency is secured. The majority of these digital currencies are based on blockchain technology.

You will see seismic shifts in the financial markets if you invest in crypto assets. The use of advanced technology has grown in popularity, causing financial systems to be disrupted. Central banks and financial institutions have the ability to alter their sway. The difficulty arises when it is difficult to classify individual crypto-assets and their impact on the ecosystem. The trend of tokens, bitcoin, and altcoins has changed the financial system.

More financial institutions are interested in crypto-asset transactions; however, fees and regulations are a major issue. To support their trading, crypto-asset exchanges must consider fiat currencies.

WHAT ARE THE MAIN TYPES OF ASSETS?

A resource held or constrained by an organization, individual, or government that is required to create critical monetary advantages is called a resource. Current, non-current, substantial, theoretical, practical, and non-useful resources are altogether normal resources. The capacity to precisely recognize and recognize kinds of resources is fundamental for the endurance of an organization, particularly its goal and the dangers related to it.

"Resources are a wellspring of command over a substance because of past occasions and when it is normal that future monetary advantages will stream to that element," as indicated by the International Financial Reporting Standards (IFRS).

A few instances of resources are:
- Accounts receivable
- Money and value
- Investment
- Goods
- Cars

PPE (Goods, Equipment, and Equipment)
Copyright (theoretical resource)
- Furniture

Resource highlights
The structure has three primary zones:
- Ownership: Assets address possession that can be changed over into money or money counterparts later on.
- Economic Value: Goods are important and can be sold or sold.
- Resource: Assets are a resource that can be utilized to produce future financial advantages.

Division of resources
Products are separated into three classifications:
1. Adaptability: Goods are grouped by the fact that they are so natural to change over into cash.
2. Regular Resources: Assets are arranged by their reality (as such, hardware, and elusive resources).
3. Usage: The characterization of a resource depends on its utilization or the reason for the business activity.

Resource Separation: Conversion
Resources are named current resources or characterized resources dependent on their capacity to change over cash. Momentary resources contrasted with long-haul resources are another method of communicating this idea.

1. Assets that are Current
Present assets that are those that can be for utilization of the conversion can be converted to money or cash equivalents quickly (typically that hold in 01-year). Current assets, also known as liquid assets, include the following:

- Cash equivalents
- Cash
- Accounts receivables
- Short-term deposits
- Marketable securities
- Inventory
- Office supplies

2. Permanent and present assets
Those assets that are not in current state or assets are the can't be converted into cash or cash equivalents quickly. Fixed assets, long-term assets, and hard assets are all terms used to describe non-current assets. The following are examples of non-current of these assets or may be as fixed:-
- Building
- Land
- Equipment
- Machinery
- Trademarks
- Patents

Classification of Assets: Physical Existence
Assets may be classified into main 02-types, that are the tangible and non-tangible, that may be depending on their physical existence.

1. Tangible Assets
Assets that have a physical existence are known as tangible assets (that can we touch, feel and hear). The following are examples of tangible assets:

- Property
- Construction
- Equipment
- Tools and equipment
- Money
- Office equipment
- Inventories
- Securities that can be sold.

Intangible Assets are the second type of asset.
Intangible assets are assets that do not have a physical location. Intangible assets include things like:

- Generosity
- Intellectual property (patents)
- Reputation
- Copyright protection
- Patents and trademarks
- Business secrets
- Permits and licenses
- Intellectual property of the corporation

Asset Classification: Application
Resources are named useful resources or non-utilitarian resources, contingent upon how they are utilized for any reason.

1. Working Capital

Practical resources are resources expected to maintain a business consistently. Working resources, as such, are utilized to bring in cash from the organization's center tasks. Coming up next are a few instances of working resources:
- Accounts receivable
- Cash
- Building
- Inventory
- Equipment
- Machinery
- Copyrights
- Patents
- Goodwill

2. Non-Operating Assets
Unused resources are resources that are not utilized in the everyday activity of a business yet can in any case bring in cash. Non-practical resources incorporate the accompanying:

- Commercial security
- Short-term speculation
- Interest rate from a fixed store
- Free space

The Importance of Inheritance

Resource isolation is basic to the accomplishment of an organization. Understanding what resources are current resources and what resources are isolated, for instance, is significant in deciding the expense of an's organization. Understanding what resources are substantial and theoretical aids in surveying an organization's answers and dangers in a high-hazard industry.

Understanding the stockpile of income from every resource, and figuring out which level of an organization's income from its center business exercises, requires figuring out which resources are dynamic and which resources are most certainly not.

Characteristics of Crypto Assets

A straightforward meaning of crypto resources is a sort of advanced resource; be that as it may, not all computerized resources are crypto resources. So how would you see the distinction between the two?

• Cryptography is used in crypto assets.
• Distributed ledger technology is required for this type of asset.
• Unlike bitcoins, you have don't idea about the third party like related issues to that of the bank crypto-assets.
• There are three primary uses for crypto assets: as an investment, a medium of exchange, and a means of obtaining goods and services.

Crypto currencies like Bitcoin are a good example of a crypto asset. Although it is widely assumed that a currency is an asset, it's important to note that, all the crypto assets are not the crypto currencies. The explanation is that assets are divided into three categories, which are known as tokens or asset tokenization. Even though the assets can be unpredictable, they are held as investments for future profits.

Bitcoin technology investment is on the rise, and it's a great way for investors to get in on the ground floor and maximize their profits. Bitcoin was the first crypto asset, but it has since expanded to include other investments in the crypto asset market.

The Nature of Assets

Legal ownership isn't the only criterion for classifying something as an asset in accounting terms; for example, if someone buys something on hire purchase, they don't own it until the full purchase price is paid. Nonetheless, the item, along with the corresponding obligation, is recorded as an asset. Similarly, even though a lessee never owns the leased item, he can record it as an asset as long as the corresponding obligation is also shown.

In accounting terms, 'ownership' usually refers to 'legal ownership,' but there are exceptions: an interest in a tangible or intangible object, or a right to value, combined with the right of possession and use, can also be considered an asset.

If a person owns the value or economic benefit derived from a particular source, that source becomes an asset for him, and he is the economic owner, even if he is not the legal owner. In this case, the most appropriate accounting procedure should be determined by accounting substance rather than legal form.

Accounting's main purpose is to calculate profits. Income generation, on the other hand, necessitates capital investment in order to provide an enterprise with the facilities it requires to operate continuously and indefinitely.

Deferred costs are expenses that are incurred but not allocated as a cost during a period. They are an asset from the standpoint of accounting. These costs are current assets if they can be recovered within a year and fixed assets if they can be recovered over a longer period.

This asset classification is necessary for calculating profits as well as displaying the enterprise's position at a given point in time, i.e., the composition of its assets and the nature of its obligations. The goal of acquiring fixed assets is to generate income from them. They aren't purchased with the intention of reselling them. Fixed assets must produce income-generating goods, or they must be used in the operations of the business.

In accounting terms, tangible assets, such as buildings, machinery, and vehicles, make up the largest category of fixed assets. Because it is never 'consumed,' land that is not subject to depreciation or depletion through use is also considered a tangible fixed asset. Buildings, machinery, and vehicles are all subject to depreciation, which must be accounted for annually as a cost. Mines, oil and gas wells, and plantations are all examples of tangible fixed assets that are subject to depletion as a result of their use.

Intangible fixed assets, such as patents, copyrights, trademarks, and goodwill, are another type of asset. Deferred expenses and debts, such as a company's preliminary expenses, are also referred to as intangible fixed assets in accounting terms.

External assets, also known as investments, are the last to be considered as assets. Fixed-income investments, investments in ordinary shares of other companies, various investments such as pension funds, housing schemes, and insurance policies, and investment properties are among them.

The Key Is to Get in Early

The crypto world is clearly still in its early stages of development and adoption. The goal of Crypto Trend is to provide unbiased information so that investors can better assess the risks and potential of this highly volatile sector, which we've dubbed the "wild west." If you're willing to take risks, you can expect to make some serious money.
Crypto currencies have a bright future ahead of them. They have the potential to revolutionize money by instilling discipline in monetary policy. Unfortunately, there is a dark side to the crypto world. It is plagued by sloppy standards, dubious operators, excessive hype, and market crashes. Furthermore, purchasing crypto currencies and the process involves very consuming process, as noted below, governments are now stepping in to try to figure out how they can take used a single pieced of the action in the form of taxes, fees, or some other yet-to-be-developed method of taking your money.
If buying actual CCs isn't your cup of tea, know that over the next few years, the majority of the Crypto Trend Premium service's

recommendations will come from block chain and other technological advancements that will change the way we do business, much like the internet has changed our lives.

Time passes, and technology advances. There were no mobile apps or data clouds ten years ago. Robots are changing the way people do business today, in industries ranging from manufacturing to drones. Face-detecting systems in China can now authorize payments, grant access to facilities, and track the movements of each individual in a smart city. We will soon be passengers in self-driving buses and cars.

Cloud-based AI services will also be available, allowing a wide range of businesses to use artificial intelligence tools. And there's even "Dueling Neural Networks," an artificial intelligence breakthrough that allows AI to create images of things it's never seen before, giving it a sense of imagination.

As we move into the next evolution of technology, there will be some serious privacy, security, and other issues to address, but as an investor, each of these advancements provides you with the opportunity to make massive gains. The thought is to get in the perfect spot at the perfect time, with the correct organization, and in the correct way.

All things considered, while a portion of the offers we will suggest in Crypto Trend Premium will be notable industry pioneers, some will be unknown, and unsubstantiated specialized offers are not on the overall population radar.

In a few years, many of these companies you've never heard of will be household names.

_____

It's tax time - are you ready for CC craziness?

When it comes to the tax implications of buying and selling crypto coins, crypto currency (CC) investors have a lot to consider. Many governments are still debating how to participate in the action - through taxation. They know there's a lot of money on the line, and they're on the verge of going bankrupt, so they don't want to miss out. There appears to be no simple solution on which all governments can agree. Should credit cards be treated as currency, a commodity, security, a piece of property, or all of the above?

Here's what's going on in the United States, for example. The Internal Revenue Service (IRS) decided in 2014 that "convertible

virtual currency," such as Bitcoin, would be considered property. As a result of this decision, purchases made with credit cards will be subject to capital gain (or loss) and investment tax treatment, as well as all of the associated reporting requirements. Given that many retailers now accept credit cards as payment, the IRS requires everyone to do the following when using their credit card:
• keep records of how much money you've spent
• Assign a cost basis to the coins spent.
• Subtract the actual price paid from the cost basis of the coins spent.
• notify the IRS of the difference and calculate the capital gain or loss, taking into account the date the coins were purchased.

This information is included in your annual tax return, and you must either pay the taxes due or claim the capital loss. The consumer's choice of "payment method" generates all of this work. This has been dubbed a prohibitive, insane quagmire by many analysts and commentators. Consider the nightmare that would ensue if you bought two cups of coffee every day with Bit coin as your payment method. It's possible that you'll need a whole army of accountants.

There will be additional issues in the United States, as four departments want to treat CCs in their own unique way:
• CCs are classified as a commodity by the Commodity Futures Trading Commission.
• The well knows SEC-as Securities and Exchange Commission considers "some" coins to be securities.
• Fin-CEN as, The Financial Crimes Enforcement Network of the Department of the Treasury has stated that "certain activities involving convertible virtual currency constitute money transmission."
• As previously stated, the IRS want to insists the treating as the credit cards as property.
So now we may suppose to have 04- different, incompatible, and proportions of the distributed prompting us that we will decide to remind you double-check what's going on with your jurisdiction's CC tax rules. We cannot guarantee that it will make sense or be simple to comprehend. It's yet including another example which includes market's "wild west" nature.

Secrets on Security: A Gentle overview to Cryptography

Consider the egg-pounding case. To start with, break the shell, empty the substance into a holder, and afterward beat the substance until you get the outcome you need - broke eggs. The demonstration of blending egg particles is known as encryption. We say that the egg accomplished a significant degree of entropy in light of the fact that the atoms are compacted (irregular state). Interruption of the cycle is the way toward reestablishing a brought forth egg to its unique state (counting the breaking of the shell). Is it truly outlandish?

It is, however, POSSIBLE if we replace the word "egg" with "number" and "molecules" with "digits." This is the thrilling world of cryptography, my friend (crypto for short). It's a relatively new field dominated by gifted mathematicians who use terms like "non-linear polynomial relations," "in addition to the described system to that of the multivariate polynomial equations," and "Galois fields," among others. These cryptographers communicate in a language that we, mere mortals, cannot pretend to comprehend.
Everything is stored in a computer as a number. A number is assigned to your MP3 file. It's a number in your text message. Your address book has a larger number of people in it. The character "A" is represented by the number 65, while the small "a" is represented by the number 97, and so on.

Individuals can see numbers with digits from 0 to 9, yet PCs can just see 0 or 1. This is a parallel framework, which uses pieces as opposed to digits to address information. Simply increase the number of pieces by 0.3 to get a decent number of digits. Bill Gates' riches, for instance, would be minuscule in the event that he possessed 256 bits of Indonesian Rupiah (one of the world's littlest divisions).

The hexadecimal framework (base 16) utilizes ten digits from 0 to 9, just as six extra images from A to F. The hexadecimal name comes from the way that there are sixteen unique "digits" in this set. This documentation is valuable for PC clients who need to perceive what the "genuine substance" of a PC is. Deal with these advanced cash frameworks, like the Euro, Swiss Franc, British Pound, etc. A number can be "costly" in these different mathematical frameworks, for example, a thing can be bought at various costs utilizing these monetary standards.

Have you at any point inquired as to why you need to become accustomed to the best numbers in school? Numerous numbers instructors, I'm certain, have no clue about the right answer. Answer: The encryption part known as open key cryptography, which uses key numbers to handle messages straightforwardly. They notice the biggest numbers there, like 2048, 4096, and 8192 pieces.)

We need to utilize code when we need to add something to something. The code is really a number, similar to a cake equation. It is trailed by a dark and conservative article with a limited scale. You will require a key to finish the encryption cooperation (some accept it as a login condition). For cryptography to work appropriately, the key utilized in the code should have high entropy.

During the 1980s and mid-1990s, the Data Encryption Standard (DES), first presented as a norm in the last part of the 1970s, was the most generally utilized source. A 56-digit key is utilized. In the last part of the 1990s, it broke into 56 hours with specific PCs costing about $ 250,000. It is feasible to break inside a day utilizing current equipment (2005).

Thus, Triple-DES supplanted DES as a reasonable method to monitor early speculation (particularly banks). It utilizes two 56-bit keys in a three-venture measure: -

1. Encrypt by using with Key 1.

2. Decrypt by using with Key 2.

3. Encrypt with Key 1.

Just 112 bits of dynamic key length (identical to 34 digits) are utilized. Any number somewhere in the range of 0 and 5192296858534827628530496329220095 is critical. Some changed the past cycle with Key 3 to make it more productive with 168-piece keys.

The National Institute of Standards and Technology, United States of America (NIST) received the Advanced Encryption Standard (AES) as a norm in 2001. The Rijndael (articulated "rhine-doll") contract was made by Victor Rijmen and Joan Daemen, two Belgian cryptographers. The AES catches are typically 256 pieces in length (identical to 78 digits). Any number somewhere in the range of 0 and 15792089237316195423570985008687907853269984665640564039457584007913129639935 can be utilized as a key. This figure relates to the complete number of particles known to man.

In June 2003, the National Security Agency (NSA) endorsed the AES to be utilized to ensure the most private data of US government organizations (indeed, to the extent of their endorsement of execution measures). There are bits of gossip that they are the ones tuning in all the telephone discussions all throughout the planet. Likewise, the association is known as the biggest numerical manager and maybe the biggest purchaser in the PC world. The NSA might be at the bleeding edge of numerous years in the public eye about cryptographic innovation, and will without a doubt break large numbers of the frameworks right now being used. Pretty much everything about the NSA, including its spending plan, is arranged for public safety reasons.

Brutal force assaults include endeavoring to encode the scrambled articles utilizing each conceivable blend.
A dictionary attack is a type of attack that uses commonly used passwords to crack text-based passwords. In computer terms, the complete number of broadly utilized passwords is shockingly little.

A foe is somebody who can profit by knowing your encoded mysteries, be it an individual, an organization, a business rival, a foe, a swindler, or an administration office. A decided adversary has a great deal of "cerebrum" and assets. The best protection isn't the foe (difficult to accomplish), and furthermore, it is superior to the most decided rivals!

A key logger is a piece of programming or equipment that records every single key typewriter. This is the best method to break the utilization of a secret key-based framework. Since they are little, work in covertness mode, and are effortlessly downloaded from the web, programming key logger programs are normal. Progressed key loggers can work imperceptibly on the objective machine and send recorded information to the client who began the security checking period. Keystroke observing, similar to every single human action, can be useful or hazardous, contingent upon the reason for the checking. Passwords, usernames, distinguishing proof subtleties, MasterCard subtleties, and encryption are largely instances of classified data that go through the console and arrives at the PC (as composed).

We will utilize the model in the last portrayal. We should imagine you have great keys, no key locks, and no locksmith that can meddle. Your windows and entryways are blocked off. All in all, how does an interloper get into your home without breaking the front entryway with a work vehicle? The foe can go into your home by eliminating a couple of miles
from the roof. This is a heist (weakness point). There are exploits in every system, organization, and individual.

After all, it's not that difficult. Congratulation on becoming crypto-literate if you can comprehend the material which was shown in this was the section (<1 % from the total number of all user, who used computers). Try applying some of your newfound knowledge to your banker or computer professional friends if you don't believe me.

"The sum total of all human knowledge is a prime number," says Stan Secrets.

"The sum total of all human wisdom is not a prime number," says the corollary.

CHAPTER SIX

Is Crypto would use in FUTURE?

What will the face of money be in the future? Imagine entering a restaurant and seeing your favorite combo meal on the digital menu board. That instead of being priced at $ 8.99, is listed as .009 BTC. Can crypto really be a future currency? The answer to that question depends on a broad consensus on many key issues ranging from performance to safety and regulations.

Let's take a look at both sides of the (digital) currency and see how traditional fiat currency interacts with cryptocurrency.

The first and most important factor is trust.

People should have faith in the money they spend. What determines the value of the dollar? Is it real gold? Since the 1970s, the dollar has not been supported by gold. So, what gives the dollar (or other fiat currency) value? Some currencies are thought to be more stable than others. The people's reliance on the government that issues that money, which ensures its "value", is what matters.

As Bitcoin is still distributed, there is no governing body issuing coins; How does a trust work? Bitcoin is stored in a blockchain, which is an online accounting ledger that allows anyone in the world to see every single transaction. The miners (computer users in the peer-to-peer network) verify each of these transactions to prevent fraud and to ensure that no money is doubled. Miners are paid for each transaction they guarantee in exchange for their services in maintaining blockchain integrity. Because there are so many miners trying to make money, they double-check each other's work to find fault. The blockchain has never been hacked because of evidence of workflow. This trust actually gives Bitcoin its value.

Let's look at security, which is a great friend of the trust.

What happens if my bank is robbed or my credit card is misused? My bank account is protected by the Federal Deposit Insurance Corporation (FDIC). My bank may withhold any costs on my credit card that I have not approved. That is not to say that criminals will not be able to produce at least frustrating and time-consuming degrees. There is almost peace of mind that comes from knowing that any wrongdoing on my part will soon be completely remedied.

When it comes to saving your money in crypto, you have many other options. Note that your exchange is covered for protection. Notable trades, such as Binance and Coinbase, have a history of solving their customers' problems. Similarly, there are anonymous banks around the world, there is an anonymous crypto trade.

What would happen if I threw a $ 20 bill into the fire? The same can be said of cryptographic money. I will not get to those coins in case I lose my fraud or my advanced login trade. I can't stress enough that it's so important to work with a reputable organization.

When we proceed further, the next issue that to be face is, scaling. Currently, this it may be a major tangle of people overseeing the massive blockchain trade. In terms of trading speed, fiat money is much faster than cryptographic currency. Visa can handle up to 40,000 transactions per second. Blockchain can handle up to ten trades per second in normal circumstances. Another game is being played, which will grow to 60,000 positions per second. The Lightning Network, as it is known, can bring in cryptographic cash futures.

The conversation would end without reference to the notification. What is the tendency of people to have common banking and spending habits? Money is undoubtedly easy to invest most of its energy in the people who love it. You will need a Visa if you need to book a house or rental car. For comfort, safety, and rewards, I transfer my Visa wherever I go.
Did you mean that there are organizations that offer all of this in the crypto world as well? Monaco currently offers Visa name cards that convert your premium currency into your local currency.

If you've ever tried to introduce communication to an individual, you understand how dreary and how well it costs probably. Blockchain buyers sell high-quality shipping licenses to anyone in the world in minutes, regardless of where they are. It is more expensive and risky than sending a bank phone.

In both countries, there are current alternatives to finance. Applications such as Zelle, Venmo, and Messenger Pay for two or three models. These systems have been used successfully for billions of years. Did you mean to start using cryptographic cash?

Square Cash is currently investing in Bitcoin, according to CEO Jack Dorsey: "All things considered, Bitcoin is basically a past buy and sell. We acknowledge that this is a game-changer in our industry, and we need to accelerate the opportunity to save time."

"Bitcoin allows more people to access the financial system," he continued.

While undoubtedly most of us currently spend money on some kind of fiat currency, the late cryptosystem protects energy. The evidence includes us. It was difficult to get a standard transfer before 2017. Bitcoin is currently covered by all the purposes and objectives of all critical business issues. From Forbes to honesty, everyone conveys their ideas.

In any case, what do I take? How Bitcoin is sensible, complete, and financially viable for people across the planet may be the legitimacy of its prosperity. This seems to be a threat to the existence of banks and large corporations. They may be forced to take the largest step in the world.

Correlation between Crypto & The Dow Jones?

The Dow Jones Industrial Average has been around for half a month after the bull fled. Cryptographic money additionally goes through a time of change. Is there an association between the two monetary nations?

As we enter every speculation space, we should be cautious about utilizing obscure terms, for example, "bull and bear showcases." The primary justification for this is that digital currency saw in excess of twelve benefits during its 2017 amazing "bull run". In the event that you had put $ 1,000 in Bitcoin recently, you would have done above and beyond $ 10,000 eventually. That has never occurred in customary stock contributing. The Dow Jones Industrial Average expanded by 23% in 2017.

When it comes to data and charts, I'm very cautious because I've learned that you can manipulate the numbers to say whatever you want. In the same way that crypto currency experienced massive gains in 2017, it experienced a rapid correction in 2018. The point I'm trying my best to make it best, when we compare things, we should try to be objective.

The new risk has astounded numerous new kids on the block in the computerized money universe. They just heard how every one of these first individuals got rich and purchased Lambos. Because of increasing expenses as of late, this market change has gotten especially clear for more experienced shoppers. Numerous individuals have become magnates for some time in view of electronic monetary structures. Clearly, they should carry one of those advantages to the table eventually.

Additionally to be thought of, as I would see, is the new Bitcoin extension toward the finish of the trade. I acknowledge that there is a great deal of force at work here, driven by the old security official, who needs the crypto to tumble to the ground. The swapping scale and energy encompassing crypto ETFs is additionally a satisfactory method to make crypto a developing degree of "genuine" organizations, as I would see.

Subsequent to saying all that, I started to ponder, "Envision a circumstance where there is an association here."

Envision a circumstance where awful news from Wall Street added to advanced cash trades like Coinbase and Binance. Could it be that the two of them kicked the bucket simultaneously? Envision the likelihood that the opposite was working, and individuals required somewhere else to store their cash, which prompted the ascent of crypto.

I expected to pause and see the non-prejudicial wilderness rec center to make an effort not to hold the numbers and stay submitted true to form. This week is pretty much as great as anybody since it resembles having two specialty units discover an answer.

For the individuals who are new to trading advanced money, exchanging has never been shut, it isn't phenomenal for cash trades. I have been trading stocks for more than 20 years and I comprehend the sensation of embarrassment on Sunday evening with the possibility of lethargy,
"I wish I could change a position or two right now as I see the expense will change a ton when the business area opens up."

This Walmart-like passage can eliminate the hot blast that can be discharged in any capacity. Individuals can utilize conventional money trades to hold their choices and think of them as overnight.

I required the most recent seven days of crypto sharing and the five latest long periods of DJIA information to discover what can measure up to a one-week cycle.

Here is the week after week tests (3-3-18 to 3-10-18). The Dow Jones Industrial Average declined by 1330, or 5.21 percent, as 20 out of 30 document affiliations lost cash.

Discovering clashing apple-and-apple and advanced monetary standards is dangerous thinking that there is nothing of the sort as a Dow. Furthermore, as the always expanding number of circles exceeds its turn of events, this is evolving. Presently, the best blend is to utilize the best 30 advanced strategies as demonstrated by the enormous market capitalization.

According to coinmarketcap.com, 20 of the top 30 coins have dropped in value in the last seven days. Does this ring a bell? The total value of the crypto market has decreased from $445 billion to $422 billion. During the same time period, Bitcoin, which is considered the gold standard's equivalent, fell by 6.7 percent. When Bitcoin falls in value, so do the altcoins.

Is it a case of coincidence or causation? How come we got nearly identical results? Where there any other factors at play?

While the price drops appear to be similar, I find it fascinating that the reasons for this are so dissimilar. As I previously stated, numbers can be deceiving, so we must peel back the layers.

Here's the big news that's affecting the Dow:
"Strong pay data sparked fears of coming wage inflation," according to USA Today, "intensifying worries that the Federal Reserve might need to hike rates more frequently this year than the three times it had originally signaled."

Interest rates cannot manipulate crypto because it is decentralized. Higher rates could lead to investors putting their money elsewhere in the long run in search of higher returns. That's where cryptocurrency might come in handy.

What caused the crypto fix if not loan costs?

This is a result of the dubious news from numerous nations about what their status will be, which gigantically affects the market. Individuals everywhere in the world are stressed over whether nations will permit them as a genuine venture.

Late gathering proof by Jay Clayton (SEC Chairman) and Christopher Giancarlo has yielded empowering results (CFTC Chairman). While they need to keep awful players alive and guarantee that the guidelines of the AML are followed, they likewise need new endorsements.

Vulnerability gives off an impression of being a connection between the two nations as far as comparative outcomes.

Markets scorn vulnerability, as we as a whole know. In any case, the vulnerability is impermanent. What may cause tension one day can be settled the following. There are likewise times when the news is exceptionally stunning that the market has been incapacitated for quite a long time, if not years.

Separating all the information and choosing what is genuine and what isn't critical.

I center around the two stocks and cryptographic forms of money since I am long on both. Consistently, there is a chance to profit. This is particularly valid for crypto, as I generally purchase a coin that has recently dropped by 30% the other day, and afterward drop another 30% the following day, however, I have the entirety of that and more inside seven days.

I would prompt exhorting however much assortment as could be expected (this shifts relying upon the circumstance). Occasionally, one awakens, the other down. It's a smart thought to have the choice to sign in to a record that has a superior day of ethical advancement. You can presumably get this in the event that you have accounts in the two universes.

One thing is without a doubt: crypto is there to remain, and will most likely build venture bids.

Will E-Commerce Based on Crypto Finish Banking Industry having Dinosaur-Style?

The bank has been from numerous points of view or another since the underlying subsidizing was made — maybe even before that. Charges bring in cash, particularly coins. The yearly duty on one pig may have been felt at the beginning of the antiquated domains, however as the realms developed, this kind of installment turned out to be less attractive.

Since the Covid occurrence, we have not just seen going to the "bankrupt" local area, (for example, who currently needs to convey "grimy cash" in the store), however, "disconnected" charge card exchanges have now ascended to £ 45, even little exchanges, like an everyday paper or a container of milk. , presently acknowledged and paid via card.

Did you realize that presently there are in excess of 5,000 cryptographic forms of money being used, Bitcoin is at the most elevated level among them? Since its commencement in 2009, Bitcoin, specifically, has had an unrivaled exchanging history. In its short presence, this advanced digital currency has seen a ton of activity. Bitcoins were initially exchanged for barely anything. The primary critical cost increment happened in July 2010, when the estimation of one Bitcoin expanded from about $ 0.0008 to about $ at least 10,000. From that point forward, there have been huge social affairs and crashes in this asset. Notwithstanding, with the presentation of "Stable" coins, for example, those upheld by the US Dollar or Gold, the shakiness of cryptographic forms of money would now be able to be controlled.

Nonetheless, before we see this new type of Crypto-based E-Commerce as an approach to oversee and utilize our resources, including our "FIAT" reserves, how about we investigate how banks have advanced in the course of recent years.

Who doesn't recollect the old CheckBook? Preceding the presentation of bank cards in 1987, checks were significant methods for moving products to exchange. At that point came the bank cards and ATMs, which made admittance to FIAT individual resources and made online exchanges a lot simpler.

The issue with banks has been that the vast majority of us required in any event two financial balances (current and investment account), and one for every business we had. Additionally, to attempt to move cash "rapidly" from your financial balance to him, he says, the spot to go universally was totally different from SWIFT!

Expenses were likewise an issue. In addition to the fact that we needed to pay the ordinary help expense for each Bank Account, however, we likewise needed to pay a huge sum for every exchange, and, obviously, we got the fitting loan fee on our present Account on exceptionally uncommon occasions.

Moreover, consistently, utilizing proficient monetary brokers (or, all the more as of late, Artificial Intelligence (AI) exchanging frameworks), every one of OUR resources will be sold, and the Banks will be the Biggest Income for our merchandise - yet not us! See the force of "OVERNIGHT Trading" to create income.

In rundown, banks not just charge higher expenses for putting away and dispatching our merchandise yet additionally advantage from exchanging our cash the Overnight circuit, where we don't see a benefit.

Five Principle of the Gold!

We live in a time of tolerance, and when it comes to money, we want more now, not later. Whether it's a down payment or a payment for those credit cards that deplete our energy long after we stop using them, the sooner, the better. We want easy selection and quick return when it comes to investing. As a result, the current crypto currency is attacking. Why invest in machine learning or nanotechnology when Ethereum is on a more advanced path and Bitcoin is a never-ending gift?
George S Clason, an American writer of the last century, took a different approach. He has given the world a final treasure - in reality - of financial principles based on what may seem old-fashioned today: warning, wisdom, and wisdom in The Richest Man in Babylon. Clason's financial advice was provided by scholars of the ancient city of Babylon, but it is as relevant today as it was a century ago, when Wall Street Crash and the Great Depression approached.

Take the five golden rules, for example. This is for you if you want to manage your own finances, wherever you are in life:

Law No. 1: Anyone who sets aside, in any case, a tenth of the money he earns to cover his future and that of his family will receive gold with joy and great increase. To put it another way, set aside 10% of your income. Not a bit. If possible, keep more. That 10% does not go on holiday next year or in another car. It is a drag-and-drop program. Commitment to Annuity, ISAs, premium securities, and other high/closed savings records - all can be seen up to 10%. Investment costs are relatively low, however, who knows where they will be in five or ten years? Also, because of the combined interest, your deposits will grow much faster than you expect.

Law No. 2: For the owner who gets a working line of gold, he tries with honesty and fulfillment. In this way, in the event that you need to contribute differently from savings, do it wisely. There will be no digital money or fraudulent business models. The terms "production" and "business" are the ones we are surrounded by. Let money work for you, but remember that the best thing you can expect from this rainbow side is basically a long draw, a lottery predictor, not a lottery winner. By doing this, this could mean that shareholders in funded organizations pay for the shares in value and have a steady decline in the cost of the shares. You can donate directly or to the property manager through unit trusts, however, read the previous Rules 3, 4, and 5 leaving one cent...

Law No. 3: Gold holds fast to the security of the savvy proprietor who plants it with the assistance of the individuals who know him. Counsel a certified and experienced monetary counselor prior to settling on a choice. Do some exploration in the event that you are uncertain. You can look at them on the web. What sort of involvement do they have? What sort of clients do you have? See refreshes. Call them first to get a thought of what they are offering, and afterward choose if it is feasible to meet eye to eye. Take a gander at the design of their bonus. Is it accurate to say that they are independently employed, or do they have an agreement with a publicizing organization for its monetary items? Prior to exhorting you on putting resources into developing business sectors or an excursion to space, a decent monetary counselor can urge you to get the essentials accessible: annuities, disaster protection, and convenience Listen to your consultant when you have discovered somebody you can trust. Accept their recommendation genuinely. In any case, audit your relationship with them routinely, say it once per year, and in the event that you are troubled, search out another person. In the event that your judgment sounds sensible, you can remain with a similar advocate for quite a while.

Law No. 4: Gold dodges the individuals who put resources into its interest in organizations or objectives that are new or unsuitable to the individuals who have the right stuff to keep it. In the event that you have top to bottom information on the food business, consider putting resources into a store that gets a piece of the overall industry. Essentially, if your organization offers a worker stock ID framework, it bodes well to utilize it on the off chance that you accept your organization has a splendid future. Notwithstanding, you ought to never put resources into a market or monetary item that you don't completely comprehend (recall Crash!) Or that you have not investigated. On the off chance that you are thinking about engaging in cash exchanging or investment opportunities, converse with your monetary guide first. On the off chance that they don't have the data, request that they give it to somebody who does. Most importantly, keep away from anything that you don't know of, regardless of how advantageous that might be.

Rule # 5: Gold flees from people who seek unreasonable profits, from people who follow the lead of professional artists and artists, and from people who rely on their own ignorance. The fifth decision carefully follows the fourth case. When you start to search for the guidance of the money to make a lot of thoughts on the Internet, your inbox soon full of "parts" that offer international businesses social than $ 999 "bar" to change it's £ 1 £ 1XXXXXXXXXXXXXXXXXXXXXXXXXXXXXXXXXXXXXXXXX XXXXXXXXXXXXXXXXXXXXXXXXXXXXXXXXXXXXXXXXXX XXXXXXXXXXXXXXXXXXXXXXXXXXXXXXXXXXXXXX If you buy a tool to delve welcome, it will take a long time to turn red. You can't just compensate for a ton of money for a program that doesn't seem to work; you will lose an undeniable amount of money in excess of your payments. In any case, you should look at the actual research of the object. Likewise, never buy a program, speculative vehicle, or financial item from an unregistered organization with a public regulator, for example, the Financial Conduct Authority in the United Kingdom.

Crypto currency: the Fintech Disruptor

Blockchains, sidechains, and mines are only a couple of words utilized in the underground universe of cryptographic money. While it might appear to be outlandish to present new monetary terms in an all-around complex monetary world, crypto currencies give a genuinely necessary answer for probably the greatest disturbance: exchange security in the advanced world. In the high-speed universe of balance tech, cryptographic money is another logical and troublesome reaction, convenient in the requirement for secure correspondence in the times of virtual exchanges. Cryptographic money recommends doing precisely that when exchanges are simply digits and numbers!

Digital money is a verification of the idea of virtual cash that guarantees secure exchanges, namelessly utilizing a distributed organization in its fundamental structure. Some unacceptable word implies property as opposed to genuine cash. Cryptographic money models, in contrast to customary monetary forms, go about as a computerized medium with no focal power. These assets are controlled, given, and endorsed by an informal organization in association with a circulated digital currency framework, known as mining on a companion machine. Effective diggers are likewise compensated for their persistent effort. Exchange subtleties are appropriated on the blockchain network under the public key when utilized, keeping each coin from being utilized twice by a similar client. The blockchain can measure up to a bank sales register. Coins are put away safely in a secret phrase ensured computerized wallet used to address the client.

In the computerized world, planning is foreordained and can't be constrained by people, associations, government offices, or monetary foundations. Contrasted with the conventional financial framework, the cryptographic money framework is known for its speed, as advanced cash exchanges can bring in cash in minutes. It is likewise intended to be reliable, support the idea of obscurity and take out any excess chances to follow cashback to its unique proprietor. Shockingly, significant elements - speed, security, and secrecy - have made crypto-coins a favored installment technique for some unlawful exchanges.

Money rates change in the computerized cash framework, as they do in reality. Since there is an aggregate sum of coins, their worth increments as the interest for cash develops. With a market capitalization of $ 15.3 billion, Bitcoin is the biggest and best digital money to date, representing 37.6% of the market and right now exchanging at $ 8,997.31. Bitcoin entered the money market in December 2017 at a cost of $ 19,783.21 per coin prior to declining in 2018. The ascent of these distinctive advanced monetary forms, for example, NPCcoin, Ethereum, Ripple, EOS, Litecoin, and MintChip has added to the decrease.

As a result of the demanding code prerequisites, cryptocurrencies are thought to observe comparable money-related norms as gold: the expense is set solely by confined store and flexibility of premium. With the consistent changes consequently rates, its drawn-out ampleness is at this point indistinct. In like manner, placing assets into obvious endeavors is by and by more for the most part regarded than the customary money-related market.

This mechanized money is a huge piece of the mechanical aggravation behind the cutting edge disturbance. This rising can seem, by all accounts, to be empowering, compromising, and dumbfounding at the same time to the accommodating observer. While a couple of business investigators may be dubious, others believe it to be a move in financial execution. By 2030, progressed money-related structures are depended upon to spend about a fourth of the public monetary arrangement in made countries. This has viably made another practice of assets nearby the standard overall economy, and advanced money will give another game plan of adventure vehicles for a significant long an ideal opportunity to come. It is possible that Bitcoin has as of late ventured out to allow other cryptocurrencies to gain a draw. In any case, this doesn't suggest that advanced money will crash. While some money-related advocates underscored the meaning of enduring governments in the economy to control corporate organization, others said the opportunity improvement at present ought to have been kept up. The more standard cryptographic types of cash, the more they research and the rule they search for - an average mystery that frustrates modernized money and sabotages its essential explanation. Notwithstanding, the deficit of these agents and chiefs attracts a huge load of thought from the monetary sponsors and changes the way where people cooperate. The International Monetary Fund (IMF) is presently stressed that cryptographic types of cash will after a short time expect command over huge banks and abroad banks. Normal trading will be regulated by the crypto stock organization after 2030, which will outfit less conflict with more money-related worth to anticipated buyers and sellers..

On the off chance that digital money is to turn into a fundamental piece of the current monetary framework, it should meet different monetary, administrative, and social necessities. To give its principle benefit to a typical monetary framework, it should be sans hazard, simple to utilize, and very much ensured. It ought to secure the protection of the client while forestalling illegal tax avoidance, tax avoidance, and online extortion. Since these are significant parts of the advanced framework, it will require an additional couple of years to decide if digital money will actually want to contend completely with conventional monetary standards. While it might now occur, the achievement (or disappointment) of computerized money intending to the difficulties will decide the fortune of the monetary framework in the coming days.

Crypto TREND

We began Crypto Currency (CC) and addressed numerous inquiries concerning this spot in the new market in the principal CRYPTO TREND program. Consistently, there is a ton of information in this market. Here are a couple of central issues that demonstrate how to get making the rounds on the lookout:

The following significant trade will dispatch a future Bitcoin contract.

The leader of the Chicago Mercantile Exchange (CME), Terry Duffy, said: "I accept our [future] agreement will be accessible for a second week in December. Furthermore, the different sides, I accept, functioned admirably."

In accordance with legitimate endorsement, CME plans to dispatch the fate of Bitcoin before the year's over. In the event that fruitful, financial backers will have a practical alternative for "long" or "short" travel in Bitcoin. Bitcoin ETF following prospects for bitcoin are likewise included with other Exchange-Traded Funds merchants.

These advancements can possibly permit individuals to put resources into digital currencies without purchasing or utilize the CC trade. The fate of Bitcoin can possibly build the utilization of advanced resources by permitting clients and mediators to exploit their unfamiliar trade hazards. This can help dealers who need to acknowledge bitcoin installments however are not stressed over its variable cost for digital currency procurement. Institutional financial backers are likewise acclimated with the fate of controlled exchanging, which is liberated from monetary misrepresentation.

CME's move additionally proposes that bitcoin has become too enormous to be in any way overlooked, as past trades had effectively shaken the fate of crypto. Bitcoin is practically the subject of conversation for everybody in businesses, just as exchanging firms, who have endured as business sectors have risen however have remained uncommonly quiet. Since estimation and exchanging are significant in obtained markets, it tends to be hard for some other trade, like CME, to decide if the eventual fate of a solitary trade is shut.

In a meeting with CNBC, Duffy said, "You can't ignore how these turn into a never-ending problem." He says "normal organizations" need to get into bitcoin and that there is an uncommon need for pressure on customers. Duffy further acknowledges that donating to institutional traders who will be sold to the public will help reduce the madness of bitcoin.

Cryptographic funds will be used by the Japanese city to grow regenerative assets in major cities.

Nishiawakura, a region in Japan, is considering holding an Initial Coin Offering (ICO) to increase social refunds. This approach is new and may require support from a government agency or private sector. The introduction of coin issuance (ICOs) has been a major problem, and many financiers are questioning whether any new analogy will be honored, especially if the ICO changes another joke or strategy. Bitcoin was not an exciting thing.

EARLY INCOME - (ICO)

We did not specify a major financial commitment (ICO) to the core Crypto Trend program, so we have to do it now. An ICO can be held by anyone who needs to start another Blockchain project with the intention of making another token in their organization, unlike Initial Public Offering (IPO), where the organization has a real object or management acquisition and requires you to buy customers from their organization. ICOs are not targeted, and most of them have shown up as a complete strategy. The ICO Authority, in turn, can raise a lot of money to fund another Blockchain project with the organization. It has never before happened that the ICO has moved the expensive cost of tokens closer to the original and then returned to the real world immediately. With natural ICOs to enter in case you know you are young and have a few dollars, there has been so much more, we currently have 800 signals transferred. In addition to the remarkable tokens, such as Bitcoin, Ethereum, and Litecoin, these tokens have a name, each of which is a digital currency, and are denominated entirely by alt currency rates. Currently, Crypto Trend does not support placing resources on ICOs due to the high risks involved.

As we said in Issue 1, the market is as of now "wild west," and we urge you to be mindful. In this market space, a couple of monetary sponsors and early adopters have made colossal advantages; regardless, various others have lost immense compensation, if not all. Governments consider rules since they need to realize all that is being done so they can cover every one of the evaluations. They are overall vivaciously owing debt holders and engaging to earn enough to pay the rent.

The advanced currency market has so far avoided various organizations with regular monetary issues and traps, and Blockchain development can handle altogether more.

Maybe the best part of Bitcoin is that its creators have chosen a set number of coins that can anytime be conveyed - 21 million - to promise it will not at any point top off. Governments can print as much money as they need (fiat money) and put their money to death.

CHAPTER SEVEN

Assets that are Digital?

"Anything that exists is autonomous, intriguing, and important to use," as demonstrated in the meaning of a PC source. Progressed assets were things like chronicles, pictures, sound, and text where the name was brought into the world during the 90s. From here on out, the new heads utilized have acquainted another existence with this time.

Blockchain innovation

Then again, actually, the new blockchain has not changed the meaning of cutting-edge assets, it has expanded the size of the term. Many progressed assets, specifically, can bother organizations overall and shockingly the worldwide market later. Cryptographic monetary standards, for instance, are right now significant in cutting-edge asset limitations.

For what reason accomplished More Digital Assets make as a Result of Blockchain?

To comprehend why PC assets have gotten so modern, you should initially comprehend why another blockchain is making another market item, if not a totally new business area. Essentially, a blockchain is a huge association of PCs that approves data on the main record all the while. Data can be erased, altered, and scrambled utilizing this association.

The degree of comprehension given by the new blockchain is limitless. Without history, this innovation permits individuals to without a doubt shows certain pieces of a created asset. Notwithstanding the commitment of pariahs, you can show proprietorship, genuineness, trade history, and area. Subsequently, the blockchain restoration presented another time of two-way trades.

Blockchain design permits you to dump the specialist. Progressed Blockchain assets rely upon the guidelines installed in the association code or which might be simply the brand. Essentially, these rules are reliably tried by the association. Since the appearance of the new blockchain, this coding has essentially progressed. Phenomenal arrangements, which are logically connected associations, are at the center of the significant asset distress today.

Bitcoin - A Code That Changed the World Forever

Bitcoin was a significant change in the meaning of the expression "PC equipment" until this point. This was the first occasion when that cryptography and another blockchain were effectively coordinated into PC programming. Fundamentally, the Bitcoin whitepaper denoted the start of the advanced reconciliation of the economy. , "We will all recollect twenty years and think that bitcoin has been a power for great as a genuine web."

Money related Crisis of 2008

Explore the state of the overall economy in 2008 to fathom the principal driver of Bitcoin thought. The overall monetary structure was in the torments of a crisis. Governments and public banks have again and again changed rules to extend their commitment. The clear dubiousness of the save subsidizes bank is a direct result of Satoshi Nakamoto, the coordinator of puzzling Bitcoin, who needs to develop a first-class economy. This new open market will have no organizational constraints.

Bitcoin - Industrial Initiation

As the possibility of Bitcoin filled in notoriety all through the planet, so did the assessment of the cash in like manner create. A couple of creators start making their own coins in less than five years. Litecoin, Ethereum, and Monero, for example, have all used blockchain advancement to guarantee their numbers. But on the off chance that these coins use a comparative development, each high-level asset has received a unique technique to the market.

Litecoin, for example, plans to be silver in Bitcoin gold, while Ethereum hopes to give originators another way to deal with reduced substance. Monero embraced an absolutely special procedure, focusing on assurance when making his mechanized assets.

Mechanized Assets As Asset Category

We would now have the option to cause an engraving on practically all that we to have by virtue of blockchain advancement. Accordingly, in advance non-liquid assets, for instance, liabilities can be sold between anyone, wherever, up close and personal, or on the web. The ability to make a token with anything accessible makes classes of complete automated assets. These new assets are at this point making. Hence, lawmaking bodies continue making changes in the guidelines for responding to the powerful action of these organizations.

Token Taxonomy

As the universe of automated assets grows, so does the yearning of regulators and monetary benefactors to perceive the different kinds of tokens open. The segregation of electronic assets into a blockchain is known as token logical classification. Basically, the financial cost will continue accepting a huge part in future business areas because the segregation of electronic assets chooses its yield and trade. Security tokens, for example, ought to adjust to security rules. In case you don't do it in that capacity, you will defy authentic outcomes. Coming up next are the 3 head sorts of tokens getting ready:

• Cryptocurrency - Traditional cryptographic types of cash, for instance, Bitcoin and Litecoin are cases of such a high-level asset. These tokens are much of the time used as cutting-edge cash. They are isolated and give reasonable goals to peer exchange, accordingly.

• Utility Token - such a mechanized asset is used to find regard and complete various endeavors inside the customary natural surroundings. Note that it doesn't mean direct ownership or interest in an association.

• Security Token - A security token is a picture expected to address an association's offer or adventure. These tokens are extensively available in outstandingly coordinated business areas like retail, security, and monetary trades.

Token Making: Changing Markets Forever

The real estate market continues to be upset by mechanized assets like security tokens. Stages like Red Swan, for example, grant landowners to check their property. The association actually worked together with Polymath to make a $ 2.2 billion trade token in the United States. Designs with tokens have many more huge advantages than traditional home arrangements. In any case, the whole arrangement measure is speedy and requires immaterial pariah affiliation. Plans with tokens can moreover be moved immediately.

Progressed items are all finished

Progressed items would now have the option to be found wherever. Token making has the impact to be used on any money, property, purchase, or opening point. In this manner, the articulation "progressed assets" will continue suggesting the broadest extent of things. At the present time, token creation is apparently the way ahead.

Digital Assets and Crypto Assets

Any resource that exists in an advanced structure is known as a computerized resource. Crypto resources are computerized resources that utilization digital money innovation.

• All cryptographic forms of money are crypto resources, and all crypto resources are advanced resources, and the other way around.

• Not all computerized resources are advanced, and not all advanced resources are advanced resources.

Bitcoin is a "crypto" money since it is a customary resource dependent on the utilization of digital currencies.

Be that as it may, numerous resources ordinarily alluded to as "digital currencies" are not planned to be utilized like money by any stretch of the imagination.

Some utilization tokens are not expected to be utilized as an interest (in principle), while others are resources with significant tokens however are not proposed for use as money, for example, crypto kitties, token protections, and gold with tokens.

Since numerous sorts of resources can be marked, "crypto-resources" are a preferable gathering over "cryptographic forms of money" to portray the entire class of digital currencies with esteem (i.e., the vast majority utilize the term cryptographic forms of money to depict all crypto-based resources, not really good or bad don't be fractional).

As of now, not all computerized resources need to depend on cryptography, so advanced resources are a general classification. An advanced resource is whatever has esteem and is computerized.

An extra computer game record can sell in excess of a level 1 record, or one skin of an exports game can sell more than another. These are not crypto resources, yet they are advanced resources.

Statement On Assets, Classification & Treatment?

Computer programming provides more freedom to engage with everyone; after that, make sure these obligations work in accordance with the sponsored insurance, public payments, market integrity, and understanding. The purpose of the guidelines is not to prevent innovation or development but to set standards that improve ethics, making the market more efficient and productive.

The Commission, as the leader in the major business sector in Nigeria, was responsible for regulating the speculation and security business in Nigeria under Section 13 of the Investment and Security Act, 2007. In line with these forces, the SEC has established three standards. Its structure, guidelines, and concerted efforts by founders seeking authenticity and authenticity will all be guided by this.

Therefore, when the speculative character qualifies as a security exchange, the SEC will manage crypto-token or crypto-coin entities.

WHAT WILL BE RULED?

1. Unless otherwise indicated the Commission recognizes that confidential crypto resources are protected. Accordingly, the provider or manager of the proposed crypto services is responsible for proving that they do not receive and therefore do not fall under the authority of the SEC.

2. By completing the basic test record, providers or enthusiasts rely on them to meet their obligation to show that undoubted resources are not protected. In the event that the Commission ensures that large resources are defensive (which may be suggested to be clearly communicated through explicitly supported segments or other published strategies), the provider or support should request advanced resources.

3. Therefore, the path to registering capital resources will take two steps: a basic inspection record to achieve the weight of the guarantee, and the completion of the appropriate registration, which may be by a supporter or supporter, or where the weight of the guarantee is not met.

4. In addition, the Commission will manage the issuance of all Digital Assets Token (DATOs), Security Token ICOs, Initial Coin Offer (ICOs), and other high-level donations based on Blockchain in Nigeria, whether Nigerian donors or sponsors or foreign beneficiaries are focused on investors. Nigerians. The collection of advanced resources will be three (3) months from the date of compliance guidelines to present the recording of the audited archives for proper registration, as required.

WHO WILL BE REGULATED?

1. Any (individual or association) playing out their commitments including any of the Blockchain-related organizations or progressed media organizations should enroll with the Commission and adhere to its managerial guidelines. Getting, sending, and sending orders for others, sellers with their record, portfolio the board, theory direction, overseer, or proposed organizations are inside and out examples of these limits.

2. The Commission's game plan will apply to suppliers or allies of cutting-edge assets (new organizations or set up associations). Exporters or donors who are new or non-occupant may need to

open a branch office in Nigeria. Passages or new benefactors, of course, will be recognized by the Commission if Nigeria and the supplier or new help have a rebate understanding.

3. In case the new provider or supporting country is a person from the International Organization of Securities Commission, the country of cause (IOSCO) will be conceded.

To achieve these targets, the Commission has gotten the going with systems.

Computerized cash assets:

"Crypto Asset" insinuates the automated depiction of the total that can be traded on the web.

serves (1) as a technique for exchange; (2) unit of record; or potentially (3) a worth store (3)

It fills in as a value store, yet isn't seen as a genuine fragile wherever. Crypto assets are segregated from Fiat and E-cash since they are not given or guaranteed by any space, and play out the above limits solely by a comprehension between Crypto Asset customers.

The going with work assets are orchestrated by the SEC as follows:

TREATMENT OF S/N VIRTUAL DIGITAL ASSET

1. Crypto assets, for instance, non-fiat non-fiat financial structures.

Exactly when traded on the Recognized Investment Exchange as well as gave as an endeavor, it is treated as an asset and is needy upon Part E of the SEC's Rules and Regulations, similarly as some other relevant portions and following rules that may be set up later on.

2. Utility Tokens (in any case called "Unprotected Tokens")

(For example, visual tokens.) These four tokens offer help to customers.

furthermore,/or organization transport

They look like products. Spot, of course,

Trading of used tokens isn't constrained by the Securities and Exchange Commission (SEC).

But on the off chance that it is made on the Registered Investment Exchange, where it is reliant upon rules.

Part E of the Rules and Regulations of the Security and Exchange Commission, and other appropriate zones and sections

to notice the guidelines that will be passed later on

3. "Security Tokens" (for example, visual tokens)

has features and security features Change comparable properties

real actual basic, associations or pay streams partake

or then again the choice to get benefits or interest portions with respect to their appearance

Tokens like stocks, bonds, and other money-related instruments depending upon monetary development.

It is seen as protection by going to the section

"Security Definition" in ISA XVII (315). Money related organizations when in doubt

Limits that join Security Token, such as using low/high/high/high/elite assumptions

Supervising/trading/administering adventure or provoking in assistant business areas

Fitting regulatory necessities will apply to security tokens.

Market go-betweens and market heads who oversee or supervise interests in the stock exchange.

Security Tokens ought to be selected and asserted as CMOs by the Securities and Exchange Commission (SEC).

Ideally, Investment Exchange or Known Cleansing.

4. Joint Commitment Funds

Crypto Asset Management, Security Tokens, and Tickets for Specific Investment

ISA and SEC Rules and Regulations. Market individuals and market delegates

Receivables and Shared Investment Providers will be affected.

SEC underwriting/enlistment is required.

Top Indications You Need a Digital Asset Management System

You should seriously consider a digital or media asset management system if you find yourself experiencing any of the following or if you can relate to any of the following experiences.

You can't seem to find what you're looking for: One of the most important features of any asset management system is a ability to search the content. Otherwise, if you can't find what you're looking for quickly, you'll become frustrated and waste time and money on the redundant effort. It will slow you down, cause project delays, irritate your customers, and cause a slew of other issues. You'll waste time attempting to determine which hard drive or archive tape contains the information you require. Furthermore, an asset management system will enable you to organize content into groups, projects, or categories, resulting in better content organization and easier, more secure searching. Content can be enhanced with metadata and other tags, allowing search results to be refined.

You only have projects saved on hard drives: Data suicide is storing content solely on hard drives. Keeping backups on multiple drives isn't a good idea, either, because you're just adding to your headaches without a management system. Will you remember which drive has the backup if one of your drives fails? The main difference between a backup and an archive is that archive systems have brains that keep track of where your content is located, whereas backups are simply backups. Archive systems should ideally be self-describing, such as LTFS LTO (open standards for archival tape) tapes, so that no proprietary software or drives are required for restoration. Additionally, storing data (video, images, audio, documents, and so on) on a different type of media improves overall durability - LTO tape is certified for 30 years of archival use.

You have a stack of videotapes on your library shelf that you have no idea what's on: Here's a suggestion if your library looks like an endless stack of tapes and you don't know what to do with them. Make a digital copy of them. All kinds of miracles can happen once content is digitized. You can look at them, edit them, search for them, store them, manage them, repurpose them, and share them. The process of digitizing video and other content and storing it in a DAM (Digital Asset Management) or MAM (Media Asset Management - typically for video content) system is known as ingest. Effective management becomes possible once content has been ingested. Your operation will be much more efficient, and you can get rid of the videotapes if you want to save a lot of space (once you have backups in place). Outsource content ingest if you can't do it yourself.

You lost content without a backup: You think it'll never happen to you, but when it does, it'll hit you hard. Hard drives fail, and if you don't have a backup, your data will be lost forever. Murphy's Law is always in effect, and Murphy never rests. You might be able to get a restoration service at best. There's a chance you'll be able to recover the content from the hard drive, but there's no guarantee. It is better in safing than sorry, so invest in a MAM system that includes an LTO archive. There are numerous cost-effective options available, with something to suit every budget.

With content on multiple systems, your workflow is disorganized, redundant, and inefficient: Multiple groups are working on the same project, but there is a lack of communication, resulting in errors and delays. There are multiple storage systems that aren't connected, and there's no central management system to speak of. Content is strewn about, and some people aren't sure where the important clips are. One group wastes time and money by duplicating the efforts of another. Another group overwrites another's work, resulting in delays and rework. Because a key decision-maker was left in the dark about what was going on, unapproved content was released. All of these issues were solved by using a central MAM or DAM system.

Inefficiencies cause projects to be late or behind schedule: Customers are yelling because their projects are behind schedule, and you can't tell them why, so you make up excuses and lame reasons for the delays. Even if you are not yet behind schedule, you are frantically searching for the right content for the project. There's no sweat with a MAM/DAM because the content is literally at your fingertips, and collaboration makes the entire process much smoother, efficient, and on time. In the end, a MAM/DAM system pleases both producers and customers.

You ship hard drives and DVD media all over the world: Because you send data on physical media all over the world, overnight couriers adore you. However, we are in the twenty-first century, and physically transporting large amounts of data in this manner is so twentieth-century. With today's broadband data services, content can now be delivered in seconds or minutes rather than days. The best part is that it can be completely invisible to your business, saving you time and money. Your courier bills will be significantly reduced, and your internal and external clients will be much happier as a result of the immediate gratification. A central MAM can securely coordinate content delivery over the internet. Because DVDs and other media can fall into the wrong hands, electronic delivery is far safer. Who can see what content is determined by a MAM/DAM system (asset or group permissions)? If you require the burning of DVDs or Blu-ray discs, this can also be arranged. Content can be automatically sent to robotic DVD or Blu-ray burners at or near customers' locations.

CONCLUSION

Protecting Your Digital Assets - Do It Right From the Start

Insurance, accidents, and death are all topics that people prefer to avoid discussing. People are happy to talk about the car or television they want to buy, the food they like, the movie they saw, and so on.

However, as much as we dislike discussing insurance, the fact remains that we buy it - and a lot of it - because we require it. We buy insurance to protect ourselves, whether it's accident insurance, home insurance, health insurance, or life insurance to protect our loved ones.

The same thing is now happening with our "Digital Assets." These are various websites, passwords, our will, policies, and a plethora of other files and documents that we are rapidly accumulating. So many things are now available in digital format, including books, music, photographs, and video. If we have photos in albums, we can scan them and convert them to digital format. Digital versions of books are now available (using readers like the Kindle). In lieu of paper, more and more agencies and businesses are sending us statements in digital formats, such as email.

What happens to all of my Digital Assets when I die or become disabled is a big question that we don't want to discuss - but should. How will my family find out what I've got and what I'm going to do with it? Even if they have my computer, will they know where to begin looking?

How do we manage our Digital Assets?

Planning and preparing ahead of time, as with everything else in life, can save a lot of time and aggravation. My motto is, "Do It Right from the Start!" People are becoming more aware of all of this digital information, and there are now companies that can assist us in storing and organizing our Digital Assets throughout our lives, as well as automatically distributing our Digital Assets on the Due Date.

www.ingramcontent.com/pod-product-compliance
Lightning Source LLC
Chambersburg PA
CBHW070304220526
45465CB00004B/1740